D1122071

Luke's Gospel from Scratch

Also Available in the Bible from Scratch Series

The Bible from Scratch: The Old Testament for Beginners
Genesis from Scratch: The Old Testament for Beginners
The Bible from Scratch: The New Testament for Beginners
Matthew's Gospel from Scratch: The New Testament for Beginners
Mark's Gospel from Scratch: The New Testament for Beginners

Luke's Gospel from Scratch

The New Testament for Beginners

Donald L. Griggs
Paul W. Walaskay

 WESTMINSTER
JOHN KNOX PRESS
LOUISVILLE • KENTUCKY

© 2011 Donald L. Griggs and Paul W. Walaskay

First edition
Published by Westminster John Knox Press
Louisville, Kentucky

11 12 13 14 15 16 17 18 19 20—10 9 8 7 6 5 4 3 2 1

All rights reserved. No part of this book may be reproduced or transmitted in any form or by any means, electronic or mechanical, including photocopying, recording, or by any information storage or retrieval system, without permission in writing from the publisher. For information, address Westminster John Knox Press, 100 Witherspoon Street, Louisville, Kentucky 40202-1396. Or contact us online at www.wjkbooks.com.

Worksheets from the Leader's Guide may be reproduced for one-time use.

Scripture quotations, unless otherwise indicated, are from the New Revised Standard Version of the Bible, copyright © 1989 by the Division of Christian Education of the National Council of the Churches of Christ in the U.S.A., and used by permission.

Book design by Teri Kays Vinson
Cover design by Night & Day Design

Library of Congress Cataloging-in-Publication Data

Griggs, Donald L.
   Luke's Gospel from scratch : the New Testament for beginners / Donald L. Griggs, Paul W. Walaskay. — 1st ed.
       p. cm. — (Bible from scratch)
   Includes bibliographical references.
   ISBN 978-0-664-23499-7 (alk. paper)
   1. Bible. N.T. Luke—Textbooks. I. Walaskay, Paul W., 1939– II. Title.
   BS2596.G75 2011
   226.4'061—dc22

                                                                    2011014915

PRINTED IN THE UNITED STATES OF AMERICA

♾ The paper used in this publication meets the minimum requirements of the American National Standard for Information Sciences—Permanence of Paper for Printed Library Materials, ANSI Z39.48-1992

Westminster John Knox Press advocates the responsible use of our natural resources. The text paper of this book is made from 30% post-consumer waste.

Most Westminster John Knox Press books are available at special quantity discounts when purchased in bulk by corporations, organizations, and special-interest groups. For more information, please e-mail SpecialSales@wjkbooks.com.

Contents

Contents

Part One

PARTICIPANT'S GUIDE

PAUL W. WALASKAY

Preface to Part One

While the Gospel of Luke is the third Gospel in our New Testament canon, it ranks first in the hearts of countless Christians. Think about all the wonderful stories that come from Luke's pen: the birth of Jesus with a choir of angels singing to shepherds, the boy Jesus conversing with teachers in the temple, the good Samaritan, the prodigal son, the poor widow and her two copper coins, rich Zacchaeus in a sycamore tree, and more! Of all the Gospel writers, Luke is the true, even self-conscious, artist whose purpose is to present a clear and beautiful portrait of Jesus. Luke writes like a contemporary novelist, carefully staging each scene and crafting emotionally affecting dialogue.

Luke even has his characters speak in a dialect that reflects a "biblical" time and space.[1] Those who first heard Luke's book must have been struck by his use of archaic "biblical"—that is, Old Testament–style—language. The characters of his Gospel speak in third-century BCE Greek[2] rather than first-century common Greek. He has intentionally placed his characters in an Old Testament setting so that after reading the last of the prophets (Malachi) one simply continues with the biblical story. Hearing his Gospel in the first century might have been something like hearing his Gospel read today in King James English.

The words, phrasing, and grammar are not quite the same as our contemporary English,[3] but we are aware that the message sounds biblical and the setting is liturgical—something out of the ordinary. Luke intends for his readers/hearers to acknowledge that Joseph and Mary, Zechariah and Elizabeth, Jesus and his disciples, are people of the Scriptures. The story of God's interaction with the world conveyed in the Old Testament continues on through their lives. These are not ordinary people. This was not an ordinary time.

Luke–Acts

It is also important to know that Luke's Gospel is part 1 of a two-part story. It might be difficult to appreciate the Third Gospel without also reading the Acts of the Apostles. The two books were intended by Luke to be read together. Acts is not a sequel or an afterthought but integral with the Gospel, and together they make up 25 percent of the New Testament. Nevertheless, for our purposes we will consider the Gospel by itself and occasionally refer to Luke's second volume as it helps us better understand his first volume.

Who Was Luke?

Unlike the other Gospel writers, the author of the Third Gospel begins by calling attention to himself through a well-crafted prologue: "I too decided, after doing considerable research, to write a carefully constructed narrative intended to enhance your Christian education, Theophilus" (Luke 1:3, paraphr.). Of course, our Christian education is enhanced as well as we read through Luke's narrative.

Like the other Gospel authors, Luke does not identify himself. Tradition has ascribed the Third Gospel to Luke the beloved physician and companion of Paul (see the last half of Acts).[4] Nevertheless, the Gospel itself reveals information not only about its characters but also about the author. He was certainly a member of the artisan class in the Roman Empire and as such was neither poor nor rich. He was on good terms with at least one member of the upper class, his patron "most excellent" Theophilus. He was both urban (Luke's second volume emphasizes the Christian mission in the major cities of the empire) and urbane, that is, he is an author of considerable sophistication—highly literate with considerable education. Luke knows Roman culture and law, Greek poetry and philosophy, and Jewish Scripture and customs. He seems deeply concerned that Christianity be acceptable to the intellectual, social, and political elite. He is also concerned that Christians understand the political and legal apparatus of the empire. At the same time Luke reminds the Christian community, which is becoming increasingly Gentile, of its great debt to Judaism. Jesus and the early church (in Acts) are set squarely in the context of first-century Judaism as it functioned within the Roman Empire. Luke understands that within these contexts, Christianity has the potential to be a universal, inclusive religion.

Luke's Audience

Luke appears to write from a Gentile perspective to a late first-century Christian community probably composed primarily of Gentiles, though Jews would have been part of this community as well. In Luke's Gospel, Gentiles have a prominent place in the ministry of Jesus beginning with his inaugural sermon in his hometown synagogue in Nazareth (4:24–27). At the same time, Luke takes a great deal of interest in the traditions of Israel—its history, Scriptures, practices, and piety. He is respectful toward Judaism and consistently describes the church as a sect of Judaism. His two volumes read as if he were reminding his Gentile readers about their own history—how they are indebted to Judaism and how they came to have a place among the people of Israel. Luke never severs the ties between church and synagogue. These ties may be strained at times, but they are never broken. The followers of Jesus the Messiah comprise a new sect within Judaism known as "The Way."[5]

Things to Look For as You Read through Luke's Gospel

Like any author, Luke has his own literary *style*. We have already noted Luke's artful use of language, by which he tells his stories about Jesus in an Old Testament tone. Luke was also fond of parallel stories,[6] doublets,[7] and pairs, especially pairing men and women. Occasionally Luke uses hyperbole to make his point, which Walter Brueggemann calls "poetic exaggeration." Jesus' admonition " 'Whoever comes to me and does not *hate* mother and father . . . and even life itself, cannot be my disciple' " (14:26, my italics) certainly gets our attention. Look for these elements of Luke's style as you read through his Gospel.

You will also note several *themes* that run through Luke's Gospel.

- *Jerusalem.* It is the geographic and religious focus of the Gospel—Jesus begins and ends his ministry in Jerusalem, specifically in the temple (2:41–51; 21:37–38).

- *Worship.* The Gospel begins and ends with scenes of worship (1:8; 24:52). Luke borrowed freely from the liturgy of his church, beginning his Gospel with a series of songs—the song of Mary (the Magnificat), the song of Zechariah (Benedictus), and the song of Simeon (Nunc Dimittis).[8]

- *Jewish Piety.* First-century Jewish piety grounds Luke's story of Jesus. Note how often in the opening chapters of the Gospel Jewish piety and practice are mentioned.

- *Prayer.* Related to worship is Luke's emphasis on prayer. Jesus prays throughout the Gospel, and he instructs his disciples that they should pray always and not lose heart (18:1).

- *Food.* "Give us each day our daily bread" must not have been far from Luke's mind as he constructed his story. Food is mentioned either explicitly or implicitly in every chapter of the Gospel. Jesus frequently enjoys a good meal with his friends (and sometimes with those who are not so friendly).

- *The Holy Spirit.* Perhaps the most important theme in Luke's two volumes is the role of the Holy Spirit in Jesus' life and his ministry. In Luke's second volume, the Acts of the Apostles, that same divine power continues to be manifest in the community of Jesus' followers—the church.

- *A Gospel of Joy!* A final, and perhaps most important, theme for Luke is participation in the gospel of joy. Jesus not only brings the *good* news of God, he *is* the good news of God! Those who are willing to participate in this good news as followers of Jesus find themselves immersed in the joy of God, which some call grace.

Luke's particular *concerns* would also be hard to miss.

- *Men and women at work together.* Luke is interested in the social interactions that occur within the Christian community where women and men work side by side.

- *Jesus' care for the least, the last, and the lost.* Jesus' ministry includes those often left out of consideration by teachers in first-century Palestine: Samaritans, Gentiles, women, and children.

- *Possessions and the proper use of resources.* Corresponding to Luke's concern for the poor and excluded is his concern about how we use the gifts that God has given us. Those gifts have strings attached. Jesus' condition for discipleship is very difficult to hear: " 'None of you can become my disciple if you do not give up all your possessions' " (14:33).

Who Is Jesus, according to Luke?

From the very beginning of his Gospel Luke uses a wide range of terms to describe Jesus. Note especially how he piles on titles for Jesus in narrating the birth story. The angel Gabriel tells Mary: " 'You will . . . bear a son, and you will name him *Jesus*. He will be *great*, and will be called the *Son of the Most High*, and the Lord God will give to him the throne of *his ancestor David*. . . . He will be called *Son of God*' " (1:30–35, italics added). The angels sing to the shepherds, " 'To you is born this day in the city of David a *Savior*, who is the *Messiah*, the *Lord*' " (2:11, italics added).[9] Just about the only title left out in the birth narrative is *Son of Man*, which was Jesus' exclusive self-designation. Finally, toward the end of Luke's Gospel, two disciples of Jesus declare that Jesus of Nazareth " 'was a prophet mighty in deed and word' " (24:19), alluding to two major aspects of Jesus' ministry—his teaching and his healing. We will have an opportunity to look more carefully at some of these descriptions of Jesus as we explore particular aspects of Jesus' life and ministry in Luke's Gospel.

Notes

1. I am reminded of Alice Walker's *The Color Purple*. It takes a while to tune our ears to her characters.
2. In his Gospel, Luke uses a style of Greek similar to the Septuagint (LXX), the third-century BCE translation of the Hebrew OT. In his second volume, the Acts of the Apostles, his dialect shifts to the common spoken Greek of the Roman Empire as he relates the story of Paul and his mission to major Roman cities.
3. It is sometimes easier to get the flavor of Luke's archaic language by reading his Gospel in the King James Version, especially the birth stories. Note such phrases as "and it came to pass," "in the days of," "before the face of."
4. There is considerable discussion among Bible scholars regarding the authorship of the Third Gospel, Luke's vocation, and his relationship with Paul. For further information about this discussion see Paul W. Walaskay, *Acts* (Louisville, KY: Westminster John Knox Press, 1998), 2–5.
5. Acts 9:2; 19:9, 23; 22:4; 24:14, 22. In Acts 11:26 the people of Antioch first apply the nickname "Christian" to this Jewish sect.
6. Beginning with two birth stories (those of John and Jesus) and ending with

two accounts of Jesus' ascension. You will need to read the first chapter of his second volume for the second ascension story.

7. Note his careful construction of the Beatitudes and woes (6) and the parables of the Lost Sheep and Coin (15). (The numbers in parentheses refer to specific chapters in Luke's Gospel; e.g., chapter 6.)

8. Look for these in your church hymnal.

9. Luke piles on even more descriptors in the book of Acts: Great One, Heir of David, Author of Life, Prophet like Moses, Prince, and Servant of the Lord (Acts 2 and 3).

Chapter One

Luke Says Hello
and Introduces Jesus

A Study of Luke 1:1–2:52

Luke's Preface to His Gospel (1:1–4)

Luke begins his Gospel with a lengthy one-sentence introduction.[1] Writing in elegant Greek, Luke replicates the kind of introduction one would have expected of a first-rate, first-century historian. The preface tells the reader much about Luke's intentions and his research methods. Read the preface carefully, and notice what Luke says about himself (and others).

He acknowledges that he is not the first to write a story about Jesus. Many others have written "orderly accounts." Bible scholars have concluded that Luke had in hand at least two of these accounts—an early version of our Gospel of Mark, which he uses as his outline, and material that can also be found in the Gospel of Matthew but not in Mark (such as the story about Jesus healing a centurion's slave [Luke 7:1–10//Matt. 8:5–13]). Scholars call this hypothetical second source "Q," from the German *Quelle*, which simply means "source" (it is "hypothetical" because it is reconstructed by extracting material common to Luke and Matthew but not found in Mark). Luke also gathered together other materials before crafting his own narrative, materials such as the birth stories, several parables not found in the other canonical Gospels, and the resurrection stories.

After collecting, investigating, sifting, and organizing his raw literary materials, Luke tells us, "I too decided . . . to write an orderly account." His may not be the earliest of the Gospels (Mark has that distinction), but because of Luke's careful research and elegant writing the Gospel according to Luke is arguably the most beautiful.

He has dedicated his work to Theophilus. We can only speculate about this person. That Luke describes him as "most excellent" indicates a real individual of high standing in Roman society. Luke uses this term one other time, citing a letter that is addressed to "his Excellency" Felix, the Roman governor of Judea (Acts 23:26). Since Theophilus is an unusual first-century name, and the name means "lover of God," some have suggested that Luke is dedicating his book to all those who love God. While this is possible, Luke probably followed literary conventions of his time and dedicated his book to his patron, who supplied him with the financial and material means to complete his literary project.

Luke's last phrase in his introduction suggests his reason for all this hard work: "so that you may know the truth concerning the things about which you have been instructed." This comprehensive, coherent, and chronological story of Jesus is Luke's contribution to the Christian education of Theophilus and to the education of all of us who are "lovers of God." Here is the story of Jesus that every Christian needs to know.

Not Just One but Two Birth Stories (1:5–45)

At verse 5 we finally begin Luke's narrative of Jesus. At this point Luke steps offstage as the curtain rises on Jesus' story.

Luke is careful to set his narrative in its historical context. "In the days of King Herod" indicates that the beginning of the story dates to about 4 BCE, the year Herod died.[2] As we noted in the introduction, Luke has given us two birth narratives: that of John the Baptist and that of Jesus of Nazareth. This narration focuses on two women—Elizabeth and Mary—whose husbands play secondary roles. These women are a study in contrasts.

Elizabeth is a woman of high status connected to the Jerusalem temple priesthood through her husband, Zechariah. She herself is of priestly lineage as "a descendant of Aaron." She is also "righteous before God" and upholds all the "commandments and regulations of the Lord." There is just one problem. She is old and has not been able to bear children, which has been her "disgrace." Now at last God has rectified this problem. She is pregnant with a son who is destined to follow in the footsteps of the great prophets of Israel.

Mary, on the other hand, is a young woman (some speculate she was in her teens) from Galilee, far to the north of Jerusalem. She is a virgin, though engaged to Joseph. She has no special heritage, and her husband-to-be is a local craftsman. Yet she too has found "favor" with God. She too will be pregnant. Not only that, her child will be called " 'the son of the Most High, and the Lord God will give to him the throne of his ancestor [King] David. He will reign over the house of Jacob forever, and of his kingdom there will be no end. . . . He will be called Son of God' " (1:32–35).

This story of two miraculous births says much about the grace of God. God's grace is unexpected and surprising. Divine grace might even seem unconnected to any particular merit. Yes, Elizabeth was a good person but had to endure decades of embarrassment and disgrace while Mary seems to have done nothing in particular to foster God's favor. In the end, both women were surprised by God. This is a wonderful time for both families. Elizabeth experiences joy as she shares her good fortune with friends and relatives. Mary's joy is a bit more muted. After hearing a choir of angels celebrating the birth of her son, she simply "treasured all these words and pondered them in her heart" (2:19).

What about the men in these stories? Of Joseph, we know practically nothing. Luke does not even indicate that he married Mary (1:27; 2:5). Luke seems much more interested in telling the story of Elizabeth's husband, Zechariah. Like his wife he is righteous and blameless. Like Mary he is visited by an angel who tells him not to be afraid. God is finally going to answer his prayer. " 'Your wife Elizabeth will bear you a son, and you will name him John' " (1:13). Zechariah must have thought, "A little late, don't you think?" He says skeptically, " 'How will I know that this is so? For I am an old man, and my wife is getting on in years' " (1:18). The angel replies, "I give you good news, and this is the thanks I get? You won't be able to say another word until your wife gives you my good news in the flesh." Luke leaves to our imaginations what happens next. Zechariah quietly returns home after his temple duties. "After those days his wife Elizabeth conceived" (1:24).

Birth Set to Music (1:46–56)

As we indicated in the introduction, one of Luke's major themes is joy, and what better way to express joy than through music. Luke captures the Old Testament love of music—think of those 150 songs of praise, the Psalms, at the heart of our Old Testament canon. It has been suggested that women sang the very oldest words of the Bible as they danced on the shores of the Red Sea: " 'Sing to the LORD, for he has triumphed gloriously' " (Exod. 15:21). Luke is in good company.

Perhaps the most famous song he recorded is the song of Mary (1:46–55). Countless versions of the Magnificat have been sung in almost every language.

It is a hymn to God, the "Savior," who has looked with favor on the lowliness of his servant, Mary. Future generations will call her blessed, the same word that begins each of the Beatitudes (the Greek word for *beatitude* can also be translated "happy," which is appropriate for this Gospel of joy).

In its well-intentioned attempt to be gender neutral the NRSV uses the term "servant" to describe Mary. "Handmaiden," the term found in the King James Version, is closer to the original Greek. An ear attuned to the Old Testament hears a harmonic echo from a hymn sung by a previous handmaiden[3] of the Lord, Hannah, who after many years of disgrace (like Elizabeth) has finally given birth to the first of the Hebrew prophets, Samuel. Read both songs and compare them (1 Sam. 2:1–10 and Luke 1:46–55).

Hannah personalizes her song as, like Elizabeth, she seeks vindication from her former disgrace:

> "My heart exults in the LORD;
>> my strength is exalted in my God.
> My mouth derides my enemies,
>> because I rejoice in my victory." (1 Sam. 2:1)

Mary moves from the personal to the universal in widening and sharing the scope of her grace:

> "My soul magnifies the Lord,
>> And my spirit rejoices in God my Savior,
> for he has looked with favor on the lowliness of his servant.
>> Surely, from now on all generations will call me blessed;
> for the Mighty One has done great things for me,
>> and holy is his name." (Luke 1:46–49)

Hannah sings,

> "The bows of the mighty are broken,
>> but the feeble gird on strength." (1 Sam 2:4)

Mary echoes and amplifies,

> "He has brought down the powerful from their thrones,
>> and lifted up the lowly;
> he has filled the hungry with good things,
>> and sent the rich away empty." (Luke 1:52–53)

Note the main theme of both songs, a theme that is very important to Luke. The birth of Jesus portends a revolution. There is going to be a new order of things with the coming of Jesus. The current order should not be taken for granted nor is it necessarily, as many thought, divinely ordained. For a moment let's jump ahead to Luke's version of the Beatitudes (6:20–23; we will compare this passage to Matthew's version [5:3–12] in a later chapter). Jesus himself echoes the revolutionary song of his mother.

> "Blessed are you who are poor. . . .
> Blessed are you who are hungry now. . . .
> Blessed are you who weep now. . . .
> Blessed are you when people hate you, and when they exclude you,
>   revile you, and defame you on account of the Son of Man."

Now read Jesus' four corresponding woes (6:24–26):

> "But woe to you who are rich. . . .
> Woe to you who are full now. . . .
> Woe to you who are laughing now. . . .
> Woe to you when all speak well of you. . . ."

It is difficult to miss the revolutionary nature (God is revolving the wheel of history) of Mary's song and Jesus' message. How would Luke's audience have heard this theme? How would they have reacted? What might this theme say about Luke's audience?

The Birth of John the Baptist (1:57–80)

The scene shifts quickly back to Elizabeth, who gives birth to her own son. The first order of business following the blessed event was the child's circumcision and naming. Zechariah had been instructed by the angel to call the boy John (1:13). The surprised crowd around her insists that he should be given the name of his father, Zechariah. When they ask Elizabeth's husband about this, a much-chastened and mute Zechariah writes the name "John" on a tablet, freeing his tongue to sing a second song.[4] The nature of this song is less revolutionary and more pastoral than Mary's. Zechariah recounts Israel's rich history—the royal house of David, God's covenant with Abraham, and the "holy prophets from of old." Now at the turning point in history God has brought from Elizabeth's womb a child who

> "will be called the prophet of the Most High;
>   for you will go before the Lord to prepare his ways,
> to give knowledge of salvation to his people
>   by the forgiveness of their sins.
> . . . .
> to give light to those who sit in darkness and in the shadow of death,
>   to guide our feet into the way of peace." (1:76–79)

Luke's typical brief transition simply notes that John "grew and became strong in spirit, and he was in the wilderness until the day he appeared publicly to Israel" (1:80).

The Birth of Jesus (2:1–40)

Never mind that Luke is a bit off in his chronology regarding the birth of Jesus. He has larger issues to address. While Luke indicates that these births took place during the reign of King Herod (37–4 BCE), he also connects the birth of Jesus with a Roman census in Judea. In 6 CE the reins of power in Judea were transferred from the household of Herod to direct Roman rule under the legate of Syria, Quirinius. One of the first orders of business when securing a new province was a census, the purpose of which was twofold: to determine the number of inhabitants in this new Roman province (what size political and police force will be needed?) and to assess taxes (to support this Rome-imposed apparatus). Joseph and Mary traveled to Bethlehem in response to the decree from Emperor Augustus that Judeans should register for this inaugural Roman census. In his second volume Luke links the uprising of Judas the Galilean with this census (Acts 5:37). Judas rejected the intrusion of the Roman government in Judea and mounted an armed rebellion that was quickly crushed by the Roman army.

Given the revolutionary nature of Mary's song, it might have come as a surprise to Luke's early readers that Joseph and Mary fulfill the requirements of the Roman edict. They traveled to Bethlehem (Luke says it is because Joseph was related to the household, and therefore the city, of David) to sign the census form. While there, Mary gave birth to Jesus.

Most Christmas pageants present this scene with a warm holiday glow— Mary cradling Jesus in the soft light of a straw-filled manger, Joseph looking on thoughtfully, and shepherds wandering in from surrounding fields to see the beautiful mother and child. Even wealthy wise men from the East, imported from Matthew's Gospel, make a cameo appearance. And then an angel appears to the shepherds while they walk toward the manger. Folks who first read this story would have been roused from the pastoral beauty of this scene and startled by some serious political overtones on the lips of the angels. The lead angel says to the shepherds (and to Luke's early readers and us):

> "Do not be afraid; for see—I am bringing you good news [gospel!] of great joy [a major Lukan theme] for all people [another Lukan theme]: to you is born this day in the city of David [Israel's royal city] a Savior [a title reserved for the emperor], who is the Messiah [a Hebrew title applied to King David and his royal heirs], the Lord [a title used by the emperor and also used by Jews to refer to God]." (2:10–11)

Luke has laid on Jesus several titles of authority that might make some in Luke's audience a bit anxious. Nevertheless he continues.

> Suddenly there was with the angel a multitude of the heavenly host, praising God and saying,
>
> > "Glory to God in the highest heaven,
> > and on earth peace among those whom he favors!" (2:13–14)

The more sophisticated of Luke's hearers might have heard in the angel's doxology an echo of the Roman poet Virgil's hymn celebrating the birth of another baby boy—Caesar Augustus.

Luke notes that the shepherds returned to the fields, telling everyone they encountered about the angelic message regarding Jesus. Meanwhile Mary keeps this potentially explosive message to herself. This secrecy would serve her and her son well . . . for a while.

Luke concludes his birth narrative with a return to the temple. Luke once again emphasizes the piety of Jesus' parents, who have him circumcised on his eighth day as a fulfillment of Mosaic law. The law also required that Mary go through a rite of purification forty days after the birth of a male child. She purchases the required two doves for sacrifice, indicating that she is not wealthy; otherwise she would have sacrificed a lamb. A pious pair, Simeon and Anna, show up to offer their blessings on the child. Simeon is delighted that he has lived long enough to see the Lord's Messiah. The Holy Spirit had fulfilled its promise. And Simeon sings a third song that emphasizes the universal scope of God's work through Jesus. Finally old Anna has hope that Jesus will spark the redemption of Jerusalem. Again Luke's readers might have squirmed, asking themselves, "Redemption from what?"

With a single sentence Luke provides a bridge that quickly brings the reader to Jesus at twelve years of age. This story probably answered a question that was on the minds of early Christians. What was Jesus like as a child? Luke offers his readers one small vignette. Other early noncanonical Gospels provided additional stories about the boy Jesus that are fun to read and are clearly fanciful. For example you might want to read the *Infancy Gospel of Thomas* contained in Wilhelm Schneemelcher's *The New Testament Apocrypha*.[5]

Jesus in the Temple (2:41–52)

Following the circumcision of Jesus and the purification of Mary in the temple, Luke fast-forwards the story of Jesus twelve years. Luke notes almost offhandedly that Jesus' parents traveled to Jerusalem every spring to celebrate Passover in the temple. Elizabeth and Zechariah, Simeon and Anna, and Mary and Joseph are models of first-century Jewish piety. Luke also notes that Jesus was not only religious but precocious as well. Jesus was so caught up with his conversations with scholars in the temple that he completely missed the exodus of his parents and their company of travelers returning to Galilee.

Here Luke is at his storytelling best. Be sure to read all the details he has loaded into this short story. Note especially the exchange between Jesus and his mother when she finally found him "sitting among the teachers, listening to them and asking them questions" (2:46). Luke uses this story to give his readers a taste of things to come. Onlookers are "amazed" at Jesus' understanding of Jewish law and customs. Even his relieved parents are astonished at this scene. Mother Mary, however, greets her son with a scold. " 'Child, why have you treated us like this? Look, your father and I have been searching for you in great anxiety.' "

In framing Jesus' response to his parents, Luke offers his readers a taste of things to come. Jesus will himself become a teacher, and his particular teaching tool will be the parable—aphorisms, similes, metaphors, and short stories. Parables have also been likened to riddles—riddles that push the hearer to think more deeply about the parable and what it might say about his or her life.[6] What follows is Jesus' very first parable, and it deserves to be read carefully.

The first words of Jesus recorded by Luke are two questions that might seem a bit impertinent coming from a twelve-year-old who has just caused his parents a lot of grief: " 'Why were you searching for me? Did you not know that I must be in my Father's house?' " Jesus (and Luke) uses theologically loaded language. That little word "must" is not your ordinary imperative—"I *must* go grocery shopping." This version of "must" is a favorite theological term for Luke. It means something like "God has ordered/ordained me to (do something)." This is a divine imperative: "I had no choice; God has commanded that I be in my Father's house."

The other fine theological point Luke wants to convey has to do with Jesus' parentage. Jesus used the metaphor "Father" (really two metaphors—also consider "house"). We know that when he mentioned "Father" he meant God—in order to be sure we get the point our English text begins the word with a capital *F*. " 'Did you not know that I must be in my Father's house?' " This is Jesus' first parable, or riddle, which escapes his parents: "They did not understand what he said to them." Nevertheless, Luke notes that his mother "treasured all these things in her heart."

As a bridge to his next section, Jesus' Galilean ministry, Luke uses a single sentence to again fast-forward his story of Jesus, eighteen years this time. During that time "Jesus increased in wisdom and in years, and in divine and human favor."

Notes

1. Note that our other three Gospel writers jump right into the story of Jesus. In the first two verses of the Acts of the Apostles Luke offers a second preface that reiterates very briefly what he covered in his first volume and leads the reader into volume 2.

2. Luke provides the reader with another clear historical benchmark at 3:1: "In the fifteenth year of the reign of Emperor Tiberius . . . ," about 26 CE. Please note the use of BCE and CE, which is the conventional way contemporary scholars assign historical dates. BCE stands for Before Common Era and corresponds to BC, Before Christ. CE stands for Common Era and corresponds to AD, *Anno Domini* ("year of the Lord [Jesus]").

3. See 1 Sam. 1:11, 18.

4. The Song of Zechariah has also been set to music and may be found in many hymnals.

5. Vol. 1, ed. Wilhelm Schneemelcher, trans. R. McL. Wilson (Philadelphia: Westminster Press, 1963).

6. We will return to this aspect of Jesus' teaching in a later chapter.

Chapter Two

Jesus Begins His Work

A Study of Luke 3:1–4:44

Luke Sets the Stage for John the Baptist and Jesus of Nazareth (3:1–2)

Luke fast-forwards his story eighteen years, anchoring it once again in its historical context—both Roman and Jewish. Since there was no system of assigning dates such as 2011 CE (or AD 2011, see note 2, chap. 1), Luke used the conventional first-century historian's approach—"In the fifteenth year of the reign of Emperor Tiberius." We would write, "In 26 CE. . . ." Luke also lets us know who was in charge of this portion of the Roman world—a cast of characters that will become part, either explicitly or implicitly, of his story:

> *Pontius Pilate, Roman governor of Judea*: We certainly know who Pilate was and his serious role in the ending of Jesus' life. We will return to a discussion of Pilate when we look at the trial and death of Jesus.

> *Herod, Roman tetrarch (literally, "ruler of one-quarter territory") of Galilee*:[1] He was from a powerful and politically connected family, the Herodians. Herod Antipas was one of the surviving sons of King

Herod the Great (1:5). Jesus calls him " 'that fox' " (only in Luke's Gospel; 13:32). Luke keeps Herod in the background of his Gospel (9:7–9; 13:31–32) until the end of the story when he reprises Herod for a role in Jesus' trial (23:6–12; again, only in Luke's Gospel). It has been suggested that among the sources Luke gathered for his story were materials about the Herodian household that he wove into his narrative.[2]

Philip and Lysanias: These are two more sons of Herod the Great who each received a quarter of their father's territory to rule. You might observe, "That makes three-quarters. What about the fourth?" Luke alluded to the fourth son in his narrative of the Roman taxation (2:1–5). After the death of Herod the Great (4 BCE) his territory was divided into quarters and doled out to each of his sons. Archelaus, the son missing from Luke's list, received the tetrarchy of Judea, Samaria, and Idumea. His rule was so disastrous that within ten years (6 CE) Jewish leaders in Jerusalem petitioned Rome to have him removed, which Rome was only too happy to do by imposing direct rule through a Roman governor.

Luke also set the ministry of Jesus in its Jewish political and religious setting.

Annas and Caiaphas: Luke indicates that both are temple high priests. Actually there was only one high priest at a time. Caiaphas was the functioning high priest, and Annas was a retired high priest—perhaps something like "high priest emeritus."

John the Baptist (3:3–20)

Luke is now ready to continue his story of Jesus, who he notes is now about thirty years old. As with his birth narrative, Luke begins not with Jesus but with John, son of Zechariah. John is in the rugged wilderness of the Jordan River preaching and baptizing (literally "dipping into water"). He calls on his hearers to repent of their sins and to show their intention to live better lives by being washed in the river. Luke notes that three groups have come to hear John: the crowds, tax collectors, and soldiers. Each group asks John what they are to do to continue their repentant lives. John has advice for each.

The crowds is Luke's designation for an amorphous group of Jewish peasants that seem to wander around listening now to John and later to Jesus. For the most part they are favorably disposed to John and Jesus. John's advice is simple and direct—one of those lessons we learned in kindergarten: "Share what you have." Live according to the ethics of the Old Testament prophets.

The tax collectors stood with one foot in Judaism and one in the Roman government. Because they represented the heavy hand of Rome (i.e., fear of "big government," even in the first century), they were despised by their fellow and sister Jews. Jesus seemed to like them nonetheless. Some New Testament commentators have suggested that tax collectors were hated because they were freelance fleecers of the public, gouging as much as they could from hapless peasants as long as they covered their tax quota to Rome. This is not quite right—which John reflects in his advice to them: " 'Collect no more than the amount *prescribed* for you' " (3:13, italics added). This conforms with current Roman ethics and law. In the old days, during the time of the Roman Republic and before the reign of Augustus and the Roman Empire,[3] the management of the tax system was auctioned off by the Roman senate to large companies in Rome. Everyone from the CEO to the lowliest tax collector wanted his piece of the pie. And then there were corporate investors to be paid. This unregulated approach led to fraud, abuse, and gouging. As part of his government reorganization Augustus brought about sweeping reforms to the tax code. He brought the tax system under the direct control of the government in Rome, placed the bureaucrats on salaries, and rationalized and regulated the assessment and collection of taxes. He eliminated the profit motive and instituted serious legal penalties for those who violated the tax code. So when John said, " 'Collect no more that the amount prescribed for you,' " tax collectors knew exactly what he meant.

The soldiers represented the Roman Empire to ordinary folk. It seems surprising that they should ask scruffy John the Baptist what they are to do to live lives "worthy of repentance." Nevertheless John has a word of ethical advice for them, too. As with the tax collectors, he also reminds them of their legal and ethical obligation to the Roman government. Don't extort money from the peasants, but " 'be satisfied with your wages,' " which were relatively good. We will return to a discussion of the Roman army in a later chapter.

The Baptism of Jesus (3:21–22)

Unlike the other Gospel writers Luke takes his time getting to his hero, Jesus. When he finally mentions Jesus, he spends only two sentences on Jesus' baptism. Compare Luke 3:21–22 with Matthew 3:13–17. What differences do you notice? First, you might note that Matthew's version is longer and includes a discussion between Jesus and John that raises a question about why Jesus should be baptized at all. Since the baptism of Jesus appears in all four Gospels (a rarity), it must bear a kernel of historical, if awkward, truth. The washing offered by John was a symbol of "repentance for the forgiveness of sins" (3:3). Do you see the problem? Mark simply reports the baptism. Matthew and John expand on it and explain it. By using the passive voice Luke almost brushes it aside—if you blink you might miss this significant turning point in the life of Jesus.

The descent of the Holy Spirit on Jesus represents an important motif in Luke's Gospel, and it is this aspect of Jesus' baptism that Luke wishes to emphasize. Note his description of the Holy Spirit. The Spirit descends not just "like a dove" (Mark 1:10; Matt. 3:16) but "in bodily form like a dove." The Holy Spirit has come to Jesus "feathers and all." Luke provides another graphic description of the Holy Spirit at the beginning of his second volume. At the baptism of the church in Acts 2, the Spirit of God descends as a "tongue of fire" that rests on each disciple. This is Luke's way of rendering tangible that which is intangible.

Luke appears ready to move quickly from this scene. But before the ministry of Jesus begins, Luke tells his reader about Jesus' pedigree and his willingness to be put to the test.

Genealogy (3:23–38)

Matthew and Luke offer the reader a genealogy of Jesus. Once again, you might want to compare the two versions. Both genealogies have in common Abraham (Israel's first patriarch) and David (Israel's first king). These ancestors locate Jesus squarely in Israel's rich heritage. Notice, however, that the two Gospels reverse each other's order: Matthew begins with Abraham the patriarch and works forward; Luke begins with Joseph (including a parenthetical question about Jesus' paternity) and works backward. Also note that Luke's list is much longer than Matthew's. Matthew, who is concerned to present a very Jewish Jesus, begins Jesus' genealogy with Abraham, Israel's father. Luke, on the other hand, traces Jesus' heritage past Israel's patriarchs, all the way to Adam, the "son of God." Luke has added a universal dimension to Jesus' genealogy. Jesus is "son of God," savior of all humankind.

By offering this genealogy Luke rounds out his introduction to Jesus. Jesus has an impressive pedigree. Angels have declared him Savior and Messiah (2:11). God has claimed him as the Beloved Son (3:22). And now, if there be any doubt, let the record show that Jesus is son of David, son of Abraham, son of Adam, and son of God.

Testing . . . Testing (4:1–13) ✕

You may have seen the poster that reads, "Your life is a test. It is only a test. If this were your real life, you would have been given better instructions."

Part of this might have been true for Jesus' life. His life was a test, and the three tests (our English translation calls them "temptations") may represent the kinds of tests Jesus felt throughout his life. First, he is asked by the devil to do a miracle just to prove he can (Herod makes a similar request during Jesus' trial; 23:8). Second, Jesus is offered authority (an important Roman political term) over "all the kingdoms of the world" (at his triumphal entry into Jerusalem Jesus is hailed as "the king who comes in the name of the Lord"; 19:38). Finally, the devil asks him to put God to the test: " 'Throw yourself down from here' "—the pinnacle of the temple. God will save you. Once again the reader is invited to look at the end of Luke's story. God did not save Jesus from death. Yes, God vindicated that death, but nevertheless Jesus died a painful death as a real human being.

Luke offers one final note that provokes the reader to remember the end of Luke's story. He writes, "When the devil had finished every test, he departed from him until an opportune time." Scholars have noticed that in Luke's Gospel Jesus seems to be free of harassment by the devil. However, when we come near to the Last Supper, "then Satan entered into Judas . . ." (22:3). The opportune and ominous time has come when Jesus will be put to one final test. But that is getting ahead of our story.

Jesus' First Sermon in His Home Synagogue Receives Mixed Reviews (4:14–36)

Luke tells us that Jesus began his work as a teacher in synagogues near the Sea of Galilee and was well received by those who heard him. We should note that synagogues in Jewish communities served a variety of purposes. "Synagogue" is a Greek word that means "gathering of people" who might come together for a variety of purposes—guild meetings, social events, funerals, and religious services. Local Jewish communities might dedicate a building that functioned as a place for community meetings, judicial proceedings, worship, and education.

Jesus, who has established a solid reputation as a teacher, was invited to return home to lead a Sabbath worship service. Worship would have begun with the congregation reciting the Shema, "Hear, O Israel: the Lord our God is one Lord," followed by prescribed prayers for the day. Then a passage from the Torah (the first five books of the Old Testament ascribed to Moses—"Mosaic law") would have been read by the synagogue president (a layperson—the religious life of the synagogue was lay led).[4] Finally Jesus was invited to read from one of the Prophets and to offer his commentary and insights. He selected two passages from the prophet Isaiah—Isaiah 61:1–2 and 58:6. As you read this passage, note its economic and political thrust. The spirit of God (Holy Spirit) is on Isaiah (or is it on Jesus?):

> . . . to bring good news to the poor,
> . . . to proclaim release to the captives
> and recovery of sight to the blind,
> > to let the oppressed go free,
> to proclaim the year of the Lord's favor.

Even this last phrase has an economic implication. According to Leviticus 25, every fiftieth year was to be a year of jubilee marked by four types of release. The land was to lie fallow (given rest); any Israelite who had become an indentured servant would be set free; all debts were to be cancelled; and any ancestral land that had been sold because of financial necessity was to be returned to its original owner. This inaugural sermon text sets the stage for what will become a major aspect of Jesus' teaching—the intersection of ethics and economics.

It looks as if Luke has skipped over the content of Jesus' exposition of the passage from Isaiah. He simply has Jesus say, "'Today this scripture has been fulfilled in your hearing.'" While we may not know what the congregation heard, we do know that they were impressed and were not willing to let him go with only a sermon. They wanted more. Here Luke assumes the reader knows something about Jesus that has not yet been mentioned in Luke's story—that Jesus was a healer as well as a teacher: "'Do here also in your hometown the things that we have heard you did in Capernaum'" (4:23). Read carefully Jesus' response to their (unspoken) request and see if you can discover why it might have been offensive to his home folks . . . so offensive that they tried to kill him.

Jesus Begins His Ministry "with Authority" (4:31–44)

Jesus was able to leave the ruckus behind and return to the more favorable town of Capernaum, where he had considerable success teaching in the synagogue and healing those with unclean spirits. Prior to the eighteenth-century scientific revolution, folks thought that disease involved wicked demons and unclean spirits that can invade the body and mind. There are still echoes of this thought in such terms as "demented" and "lunatic" ("moonstruck"). Today we ascribe most illnesses to viruses, bacteria, and other system stressors that can be dealt with medically, psychologically, and pharmacologically. People of the first century assumed that each person had his or her own personal demon, which was thought to be a protective spirit that kept one in reasonably good health. Notice that the sick man in the synagogue (4:33) had an *unclean* demon. His personal spirit had turned on him, making him ill. In the thought world of the first century, after the unclean spirit had left the man, a good spirit would take its place, returning his body to good health.[5]

As the next vignette shows, the cause of illness was not always consigned to the spirit world. There were such rudimentary diagnoses as feeling a person's forehead for signs of a fever. In the case of Peter's mother-in-law Jesus rebukes her fever, and it leaves. In an uncharacteristic move Luke notes that she immediately got out of bed and "began to serve" the group gathered in Simon's house. Some commentators have noted that this seems to fly in the face of Luke's usual protofeminist tendencies. On the other hand, one of his messages for the reader has to do with hospitality—how to be a good host *and* how to be a good guest.

Luke uses these healing episodes to emphasize the authority of Jesus. Just as at Jesus' birth an angel had proclaimed Jesus to be a Savior, the Messiah, the Lord (2:11), so now as an adult even unclean demons grudgingly acknowledge that he is Son of God, the Messiah (4:41).

Luke concludes Jesus' successful work in Capernaum by having him say to crowds who urge him to stay, " 'I must proclaim the good news of the kingdom of God to the other cities also; for I was sent for this purpose' " (4:43). With that Jesus begins his peripatetic ministry of teaching and healing.

Notes

1. Galilee lies north of Judea. This might be a good time to get our bearings by looking at a map of first–century Palestine. Most Bibles have a set of maps near the back of the book.
2. The curious reader can find further references to the household of Herod in Luke's second volume. Luke narrates the awful death of Herod Agrippa I (grandson of Herod the Great; Acts 12) and the encounter between Paul and Herod Agrippa II (Herod's great–grandson) during Paul's trial at the end of the book of Acts (25–26).
3. Augustus began his reign in 27 BCE.
4. Pharisees, who were lay leaders, were in charge of the teaching aspect of synagogues. We will return to a discussion of their role in a later chapter.
5. The classic study of perceptions about demons and illness in antiquity is E. R. Dodds, *Pagan and Christian in an Age of Anxiety* (Cambridge: Cambridge University Press, 1965).

Chapter Three

Jesus the Healer and Jesus at Work in Galilee

A Study of Luke 5:1–9:50

In reading Luke's Gospel you will note that Luke often mixes together two aspects of Jesus' work—healing and teaching. These two aspects of Jesus' vocation are impossible to separate. Jesus is a healing teacher and a teaching healer. In this chapter we will focus on Jesus as healer. The next chapter of this study will concentrate on his work as a teacher.

Six Short Stories: Luke's Introduction to Jesus' Work (5:1–6:11)

Luke begins this section by stringing together six short stories that introduce the reader to the style and substance of Jesus' ministry. To paraphrase, Luke tells us, "This is my take on Jesus, who had a very interesting approach to life and its problems. He was not your run-of-the-mill teacher-healer. If you'd like more conventional responses to life's problems, keep looking. He is not your man."

Note the first word (or words) of each episode (as in the NRSV):

5:1—"Once"

5:12—"Once"

5:17—"One day"

5:27—"After this"

6:1—"One sabbath"

6:6—"On another sabbath"

These introductory words remind us that Luke is telling a story in the idiom of Old Testament narrative that often strings together episodes with a phrase like "and it came to pass." Older translations such as the King James Version maintained this more "biblical" voice, which was also Luke's intention.[1] More important than style is the substance of each of these six stories. Notice what Jesus does in each short story.

Story One: A Nature Miracle (5:1–11)

Jesus "sat down"—the traditional posture of a teacher before his students—"and taught the crowds." He is outdoors in a boat—a nontraditional venue for teaching. He teaches anyone who cares to listen. We are introduced to Peter, James, and John, who operate a small fishing company and will soon comprise the inner circle of Jesus' students (which is what the term "disciple" means).

When Peter complains that they have fished all night without a bite, Jesus instructs them to go deeper. This instruction becomes a parable in narrative form. Peter and company come back to shore with nets bulging with fish. But Jesus is not finished with them. He says in his typical parabolic fashion, "'From now on you will be catching people'" (5:10). Luke concludes this scene with a phrase that will become familiar to the reader: "They left *everything* and followed him" (5:11, italics added). Jesus has gathered from the crowd by the seashore his first dedicated (and impulsive?) students. In a later chapter we will look more closely at what it meant to devote oneself fully to a teacher.

Story Two: A Healing Miracle with an Orthodox Conclusion (5:12–16)

A leper has come to Jesus begging to be made clean. While we might quibble about the element of choice in Jesus' response (might he have chosen *not* to heal the man?), there is no doubt about Jesus' orthodoxy in ordering the man to show himself to the priest "'as Moses commanded'" and to make an offering as gratitude to God for his cleansing (5:14). Luke also tells us that Jesus' reputation as a teacher and healer made him exceedingly popular among the masses, so much so that he had to hide out just to get some rest.

Story Three: A Healing Miracle with an Unorthodox Conclusion (5:17–26)

Jesus is teaching in the presence of his peers, "Pharisees and teachers of the law." While Jesus is talking, the tiles of the roof overhead are removed, and a paralyzed man is slowly lowered to the ground before him. Jesus, seeing the man's physical condition, says, " 'Friend, your sins are forgiven' " (5:20). Those engaged in maintaining the traditions of Moses are offended. " 'Who can forgive sins but God alone?' " But Jesus claims to be the Son of Man with authority to forgive sins. With that Jesus says to the paralyzed man, " 'Stand up and take your bed and go to your home.' " He does as he is told, and the crowd is amazed, saying, " 'We have seen strange things today' " (5:26). There are two elements in this little story that deserve further comment: what does "Son of Man" mean and what is the connection between sin and sickness?

The phrase "Son of Man" had at least two meanings in first-century Judaism. It was a common Aramaic idiom used in the place of a personal pronoun. When Jesus says, " 'The Son of Man has nowhere to lay his head,' " he simply means "*I* have nowhere to sleep" (9:58).[2] The phrase refers to a human being. On the other hand the phrase can refer to a divine being sent by God at the end of time to establish a righteous, everlasting, and universal kingdom—the heavenly Son of Man mentioned by the prophet Daniel (Dan. 7:13; compare Dan. 8:17). And finally, "Son of Man" is the phrase that Jesus most often uses of himself in the Gospels—his exclusive self-designation.[3] Of course the difficult question is, what did he mean by referring to himself as the "Son of Man"?

The second issue raised in this story has to do with the link between sin and sickness. There was an assumption in antiquity that a person's physical condition could mirror his or her spiritual condition, an assumption that undergirds this story. The man has sinned and therefore is paralyzed. Jesus forgives his sin, and as a consequence the paralysis is lifted. If we can jump outside the Gospel of Luke for a moment and consider a healing story from John's Gospel, we might bring clarity to the issue. In John 9 Jesus heals a man who had been blind from birth. Jesus' disciples ask him, " 'Who sinned that he was born blind? This man or his parents?' " Jesus offers a wise answer to his students: " 'Neither this man nor his parents sinned; he was born blind so that God's works might be revealed in him' " (John 9:2–3). Jesus has broken the bond between sin and sickness. A person's physical condition, healthy or ill, can reveal God at work in that person. And breaking that bond relieves much of the guilt often associated with the illness of a loved one—or with our own fragility.

Jesus forgives. Jesus heals. He seems less concerned about the past than he is about the future.

Story Four: Jesus Dines in Questionable Company (5:27–39)

The Pharisees and scribes complain that Jesus has accepted an invitation to eat with "tax collectors and sinners"—a catchall phrase for those who intentionally flout Mosaic law. Pharisees and scribes would naturally have been concerned. Pharisees were lay teachers in the synagogues whose task it was to bring the law of Moses into everyday life, to help ordinary folks know how to live a life that might bring them closer to God. The most famous Christian Pharisee was Paul of Tarsus, our apostle Paul. The scribes were professional scholars of the law dedicated to a deep understanding of Scripture and passing on that understanding to eager students. Not only do these scribes and Pharisees complain to Jesus that he is eating with those who have little regard for the traditions of Moses, but they also complain that Jesus is unlike John and his disciples, who were more rigorous in seeking God's will. Jesus seems rather lax about that goal. Then Jesus begins to teach the teachers using his typical didactic tool—the parable. How might the Pharisees and scribes have responded to this parable of New and Old Wine?

Story Five: Jesus Again Pushes the Boundaries (6:1–5)

When Jesus is hungry, he eats, even if it means breaking the law by working on the Sabbath to find food. This very short story leads to a punch line that tells us a bit more about Jesus' authority: " 'The Son of Man is lord of the sabbath' " (6:5).

Story Six: Jesus Teaches and Heals on the Sabbath—This Is Going Too Far (6:6–11)

In this healing episode Jesus goes to the heart of Mosaic law. What is its purpose? To do good or to allow harm? The answer should be self-evident and calls into question a rank-ordering of goods. Just as the Son of Man is lord of the Sabbath, so is Sabbath observance subservient to good deeds. According to Luke those who were responsible for maintaining good order were not happy to find their good order reversed. What to do?

Jesus Establishes His Inner Circle of Students and Teaches Them Lessons for Life (6:12–49)

An interesting feature of Luke's Gospel is his differentiation between Jesus' disciples and apostles (6:13). Jesus had many disciples, but of this vast group he selected twelve (what is so special about that number?) to be his inner circle of students: "Come, sit at the front of the class." Luke identifies each one by name. See if his list corresponds with the inner circle mentioned in the other Gospels. While the Gospel of John mentions "the twelve," I have only been able to identify seven by name. Also notice that Luke foreshadows a dark future by describing Judas as "a traitor."

Jesus' first order of business with his new inner circle of students, and with "a great crowd of his disciples," is to teach them lessons for life. At this point it might be helpful to compare Luke's "Sermon on the Plain" with Matthew's "Sermon on the Mount" (Matthew 5–7). What differences do you detect in the setting of each "sermon?" Is what follows really a sermon? Now read the first lesson from Jesus—the "Beatitudes" (Luke 6:20–23//Matt. 5:3–12). Matthew's Jesus offers nine beatitudes. Luke records only four. Notice how crisp, to the point, and personal Luke renders Jesus' beatitudes while Matthew seems to spiritualize them:

Luke	Matthew
"Blessed are *you who are poor*,	"Blessed are *the poor* in spirit,
for *yours* is the kingdom of God.	for *theirs* is the kingdom of heaven."
"Blessed are you who are hungry now,	"Blessed are those who hunger and thirst for righteousness,
for *you* will be filled."	for *they* will be filled."

What approach to his audience does Jesus take in each Gospel? What might these beatitudes say about those who are listening to Jesus in Luke? In Matthew?

While Luke has fewer beatitudes than Matthew, he also adds four "woes" that correspond to each of the beatitudes. Luke likes symmetry.

> "Woe to you who are rich,
>   for you have received your consolation.
> "Woe to you who are full now,
>   for you will be hungry."

Following the beatitudes and woes, Luke offers five more examples of the content of Jesus' teaching. Each example begins with a simple statement, very much like a topic sentence at the head of a paragraph.

"Love your enemies" (6:27).

"Do not judge" (6:37).

"Can a blind person guide a blind person?" (6:39).

"No good tree bears bad fruit" (6:43).

"Why do you call me 'Lord, Lord,' and do not do what I tell you?" (6:46).

Read each of these examples and notice how often he uses metaphors to illustrate his point. We will return to Jesus' use of metaphors, similes, and parables in the next chapter.

Luke makes it clear that we have reached the end of this didactic section: "After Jesus had finished all his sayings in the hearing of the people, he entered Capernaum." Now that the reader knows some of the content of his teaching, Luke is ready to focus on the effects of his healing.

Jesus the Healer (7:1–8:56)

Chapters 7 and 8 round out the portion of Luke's Gospel devoted to Jesus' work in Galilee. Much of the material in these two chapters deals with Jesus the wonder worker, with five healing stories and one nature miracle ("even the winds and the water . . . obey him"; 8:22).

Perhaps the best way to begin our consideration of this part of the Gospel is by looking at a story that Luke seems to have inserted into his narrative—the conversation between Jesus and the disciples of John the Baptist. The key question from John is this: "'Are you the one who is to come [e.g., the Messiah], or are we to wait for another?'" (7:19). The repetition of this question in the next verse should be a clue about its importance. At this point Luke inserts an editorial comment: "Jesus had just then cured many people of diseases, plagues, and evil spirits, and given sight to many who were blind." And now Luke records Jesus' important answer to John and his disciples.

> "Go and tell John what you have seen and heard: the blind receive their sight, the lame walk, the lepers are cleansed, the deaf hear, the dead are raised, the poor have good news brought to them. And blessed is anyone who takes no offense at me." (7:22–23)

What has the reader already observed? Jesus has brought back to life a Roman centurion's beloved slave[4] and the only son of a widow (7:1–17; note Luke's typical pairing of male and female). In short order there will be three additional healings—a demon-possessed man is cured, the daughter of synagogue president is raised from her deathbed, and a woman who has been hemorrhaging for twelve years is made well (8:26–56). By now it is clear that Jesus *is* "the one who is to come." But before we move along we need to take a closer look at the last two healing stories.

First of all notice the structure of these stories. One is inserted into the other. Luke begins with Jairus, whose twelve-year-old daughter is dying. As Luke's literary camera quickly zooms out, we see Jesus surrounded by crowds of people. Among those pressing in on him is a woman who reaches out to touch him. When she makes contact, power goes out from Jesus, and her twelve-year bout with bleeding stops. Jesus declares, "'Daughter, your faith has made you well; go in peace'" (8:48).

Luke's literary camera zooms back in on the story of Jairus and his dying daughter. After Jairus is informed that his daughter has indeed died, Jesus tells him, "'Do not fear. Just have faith, and she will be rescued from death.'"[5] Notice the difference in response to Jesus between the woman in the previous story and the cast of characters in this story. The woman trembles and falls down before Jesus; Jesus' disciples and the girl's parents mock him. Nevertheless the outcome is positive for both "daughters."[6] It's time to celebrate: "'Give her something to eat.'"

Jesus the Life of the Party (7:36–50; 9:12–17)

We mentioned in the introduction that in every chapter of Luke's Gospel there is a reference to food. Have you noticed this? Now let's go back for a moment to Jesus' comments about John the Baptist that seem to put John in his place. "'Among those born of women no one is greater than John; yet the least in the kingdom of God is greater than he'" (7:28). Might this reflect competition between the disciples of John and the disciples of Jesus during Luke's time? Luke follows this comment with his own editorial flashback. Might we be hearing two voices (Jesus' and Luke's) in the next comment about John and his movement?

> "To what then will I compare the people of this generation? . . . They are like children sitting in the marketplace and calling to one another,
>
> > 'We played the flute for you, and you did not dance;
> > we wailed, and you did not weep.'"

Some kids are having fun while others refuse to join in the game. Spoilsports. John was an ascetic—no bread, no wine, no fun: "'He has a demon!'" Jesus was the life of the party—eating, drinking, living it up with sinners: "'A glutton and a drunkard.'"

You can't win this one. Luke concludes, "Wisdom is vindicated by all her children"—both the straitlaced and the fun lovers. Think about that.

It should come as no surprise that the very next scene is a dinner party. It does come as a surprise, however, that a woman of the streets crashes the party to find the life of the party. Read Luke's almost embarrassingly sensuous description of the woman's actions. Luke is not reticent in telling us one of the most beautiful stories in the New Testament—a story rendered all the more elegant by the contrasting responses of Simon and Jesus. Simon thinks to himself, "Surely Jesus knows what kind of woman is caressing his feet." Jesus responds with a short parable about the canceling of debts—a person with great debt has a great deal of love toward the one who has graciously forgiven the debt. The woman has treated Jesus with more respect and attention than did Simon. In fact she did what Simon, if he were a good host, should have done. Who is the real host of this feast? The question is complicated all the more by Jesus' final benediction: " 'Go in peace' "—the farewell words of a host to his guests as they go out into the night.

As we approach the end of Jesus' time in Galilee, Luke presents Jesus as the host of his own dinner party for thousands who have gathered to hear his teaching (9:12–17). As it neared suppertime the disciples became anxious. " 'Send the crowd away,' " they said. But Jesus instructed his disciples, " 'You give them something to eat.' They said, 'We have no more than five loaves of bread and two fish." Taking that gift, Jesus "looked up to heaven, and *blessed* and *broke* [the loaves], and *gave* them to the disciples to set before the crowd. And all ate and were filled" (italics added). Note the words in italics—he blessed, he broke, he gave. Do they remind you of anything? They certainly would have reminded Luke's first readers of the last great meal Jesus had with his disciples—a meal that Jesus still shares with his disciples.[7]

" 'Who do you say that I am?' " (9:18–50)

At 9:18 Luke again uses the biblical *"kai egeneto"*—"Once [upon a time]." This signals a major shift in theme. " 'Who do the crowds say that I am?' " asks Jesus. They tell him that some say he is John the Baptist;[8] others, that he is the Old Testament prophet Elijah; " 'and still others, that one of the ancient prophets has arisen.' " Then Jesus asks his inner circle of disciples—and it is the question we readers must answer: " 'But who do you say that I am?' " Peter is quick to answer: " 'The Messiah of God.' "

Why did Jesus respond the way that he did? Why did he immediately shift from Messiah-talk to "Son of Man"? What were the personal and political implications for Jesus? Jesus tells his disciples what will happen to him—the first of three predictions of his passion.[9] The disciples who expected him to be a messiah—that is, a royal figure—must have been confused with Jesus' talk about suffering, rejection, and death. What sort of king predicts that for himself? The confusion is further compounded as his inner circle of disciples—Peter, James, and John—experience a theophany, what we call the transfiguration. Notice the details that reflect a divine presence in this setting (9:28–36). Finally there is a divine voice from heaven that proclaims, " 'This is my Son, my Chosen; listen to him!' " Suddenly the disciples are alone with Jesus, and they remain silent about their experience.

A second time Jesus predicts his passion. The disciples, oblivious to this possibility, begin to argue about who is the best student. In typical fashion, Jesus turns things upside down. " 'The least among *all* of you [including the child at his side?] is the greatest' " (9:48, italics added). Hummm.

Next stop, Jerusalem.

Notes

1. The ancient Greek Old Testament, Luke's Bible, used the stock phrase *kai egeneto*. It was an anachronistic phrase for the first century, but Luke was writing in a self-consciously old-fashioned (third-century BCE) biblical style.
2. Also see Psalm 8:4: "What is man that thou art mindful of him, and the son of man that thou dost care for him?" (RSV).
3. The phrase is found in the New Testament most often in the Synoptic Gospels (Matthew, Mark, and Luke), but rarely outside the Gospels. Modern New Testament translators use "son of man" (lowercase "s" and "m") and "Son of Man" to distinguish between the two uses. In the Greek text there is no such distinction, and therefore it is sometimes difficult to know which meaning Jesus had in mind.
4. Compare this centurion with another that Luke presents in his second volume, Acts 10:1–2. Observe the high praise Luke heaps upon both men. Also note the mutual respect in the conversation between Jesus and the centurion (through his friends) in Luke 7:6–9, which ends in Jesus' startling declaration: " 'Not even in Israel have I found such faith.' " Finally, compare a similar story in Matthew's Gospel, 8:5–13. How might you account for the difference between Matthew and Luke in the way they present the physical distance between Jesus and the centurion?
5. 8:50. Author's translation.
6. The reader might also notice other details that link these two stories; for example, "twelve years" and Jesus' willingness to be involved with "unclean" situations.
7. It is ironic that Luke records only one of Mark's two mass-feeding stories (Mark 6; 8)—the first is in a Jewish context and the second is for Gentiles. Luke, who usually likes to tell double stories, misses Mark's theological nuance by telling only one of his feeding stories.
8. Luke earlier noted in an almost offhanded way John's beheading (9:9). Compare Mark's elaborate description (6:14–29).
9. 9:21–22; 9:43–45; 18:31–33.

Chapter Four

Jesus the Teacher
and His Journey to Jerusalem

A Study of Luke 9:51–19:27

This portion of Luke's Gospel is unique among the Gospels. You may recall that Luke used Mark as a source and outline for his story. Here Luke has inserted a ten-chapter travel narrative into Mark's outline. Jesus is on a hundred-mile trek from north to south—from Galilee to Jerusalem (you might consult a map to trace this journey). Note how often in Luke's Gospel (and in Acts) Luke talks about being "on the way." Along the way Jesus instructs by word and deed what God is like, what pleases God, and what it means to be a follower of Jesus. The previous chapter of this study focused on Jesus the healer. This chapter looks closely at Jesus the teacher who used a particular teaching tool—the parable.

Jesus, according to Luke, was a remarkable teacher. He was honored as a rabbi who interpreted the Law. Like the rabbis, he taught in synagogues, had a select group of students, and entered into debate about points of the Law with other teachers.

Yet his style differed from that of other teachers. He taught outdoors to anyone who would listen. He engaged many people whom other teachers might ignore—women, Samaritans, tax collectors, and assorted sinners. Other rabbis might pass on lessons they cherished from their teachers, but Jesus taught with his own unique authority, and he taught with a strong and commanding presence. As we have already seen, he was not afraid to challenge other teachers—you might want to jump ahead and read about his encounter with scribes who asked him about paying taxes to Caesar (20:20–26).

We have noted that his peculiar tool for teaching was the parable.[1] Almost every example of Jesus' teaching is in the form of a parable. Remember Jesus' first recorded words: " 'Did you not know that I must be in my Father's house?' " (2:49). That is a parable.

The ordinary dictionary definition of *parable* is something like this: "*n.* a simple story illustrating a moral or religious lesson."[2] In considering Jesus' teaching style we should probably expand this definition. As you read this section of Luke's Gospel, notice how often Jesus uses metaphors ("*Father*, hallowed be your name") and similes ("the kingdom of God *is like* . . . a grain of mustard seed . . . leaven" [13:18ff.]). But it is Jesus' stories that we remember most readily and fondly. Before we look specifically at some of Jesus' stories, consider this. The parable is much more than an illustration to help one live ethically. It has no right or wrong interpretation. The parable itself is a mode of religious experience that encourages the hearer to delve more deeply into his or her own spiritual consciousness. Jesus invites us into his stories in order to consider what it means to be a person of faith under the rule of God.

"He set his face . . . to Jerusalem" (9:51–62)

Luke begins this section of his book with a transitional sentence that describes the next ten chapters. "When the days drew near for him to be taken up, he set his face to go to Jerusalem" (9:51). This sentence is enigmatic on two counts. What does "taken up" mean, and why the odd phrase "set his face"?

"Taken up" might carry a note of foreboding about the destiny that awaits Jesus in Jerusalem. He will be taken up—on a cross. "Taken up" might also forecast the triumphant finale of Luke's story—Jesus will ascend into heaven.

"Set his face" is one of those antiquated phrases that Luke borrowed from his Greek version of the Old Testament. The prophet Ezekiel often uses it in his prophecies of doom. God will mete out divine punishment against those cities and nations that have attempted to thwart God's will.[3] Of particular interest is Ezekiel's prophecy regarding Jerusalem (21:2ff.). God says to Ezekiel, " 'Son of man [!], set your face toward Jerusalem and preach against the sanctuaries' " (21:2 RSV). What might Luke have had in mind when he wrote that Jesus, the son of man, "set his face to go to Jerusalem"? Note that Luke emphasized this odd phrase by repeating it (9:53).

Jesus and Prayer (10:21–22; 11:1–4)

By now you have noticed how often Luke portrays Jesus praying: at his baptism (3:21), when choosing his disciples (6:12), at the transfiguration (9:28). Jesus tells his disciples that they should pray always and not lose heart (18:1). In this section you will read the parable about the prayer of the Pharisee and the prayer of the tax collector (18:9–14).

Before beginning his teaching mission Jesus offers a prayer: "Jesus rejoiced in the Holy Spirit and said, 'I thank you, Father, Lord of heaven and earth.'" Read the rest of this prayer. "'No one knows who the Son is except the Father, or who the Father is except the Son and anyone to whom the Son chooses to reveal him'" (10:21–22; this might remind you of another important prayer of Jesus recorded in the Gospel of John, chapter 17).

A few verses later we hear another prayer of Jesus that also sounds familiar. Read Luke's version of the Lord's Prayer (11:2–4, italics added; also compare Matthew 6:9–13).

> "Father, hallowed be your name.
> Your *kingdom* come.
> Give us each day our *daily bread.*
> And forgive us our sins,
>   for we ourselves forgive everyone *indebted* to us.
> And do not bring us to the *time of trial.*"

How might the Jewish peasants who heard Jesus' prayer have understood the message in his prayer? The words in italics are themes that run through this portion of Luke's Gospel. "Kingdom" has to do with living under God's rule, which may conflict with Roman rule, especially when it comes to justice for all. "Daily bread" is basic to human existence; in order to live, every human being needs bread (remember Luke's emphasis on eating). "Indebted" was endemic to peasant existence in the Roman Empire of Jesus' time; Christians were challenged to change the economic rules. Finally and ironically, Jesus himself will soon be brought to his own "time of trial" before a representative of the Roman Empire. Again, how might peasants living in the Roman Empire have heard this prayer? How do we hear this prayer?

Jesus' First Parable on the Way: The Good Samaritan (10:25–37)

Now that Jesus has established the proper attitude to hear his stories, he tells a tale about a fellow traveler, the beloved parable of the Good Samaritan. This story is prompted by a question from a lawyer who personally and professionally is interested in living an ethical life. He wants to cut to the chase: "'What must I do to inherit eternal life?' " Like any good teacher Jesus answers the question with a question—a question that does not require much lawyerly acumen. " 'What is written in the law?' " The short answer will do: love God; love your neighbor. That's it. That's all there is to it: " 'Do this, and you will live.' "

But some lawyers do not know when to keep quiet (to put it politely). " 'And who is my neighbor?' " is his retort. So Jesus tells a story, which you can now read. Notice the first two types of people who encounter the severely wounded man: a priest and a Levite. Of all people these folks should realize that this is an opportunity to "love your neighbor."[4]

Jesus is telling a well-known folk tale. His hearers have heard this one before, and they know what's coming—at least they think they know. A third person will come along and actually offer aid to the wounded man. She is an *Israelite*, an ordinary unsophisticated Jewish peasant. She may not know the Law, but she will honor the Law by helping him out of the goodness of her heart. Here Jesus pulls a fast one. " 'But a Samaritan while traveling came near him; and when he saw him, he was moved with pity' " (10:33). Did he just say what I think he said? A Samaritan? This flies in the face of conventional Jewish attitudes toward Samaritans, who were not looked upon fondly by those who were following Jesus. Samaritans were social outcasts even for Jewish peasants. For a historical (that is, Old Testament) account of these people read 2 Kings 17:24–34 (also see John 4:7–9). Nevertheless, in Jesus' version of the story this unnamed Samaritan not only comes to the man's aid but does so with extravagance. He tells the innkeeper, " ' "Take care of him; and when I come back, I will repay you whatever more you spend." ' "

Jesus turns back to the lawyer. " 'Which of these three, do you think, was a neighbor to the man who fell into the hands of the robbers?' " With embarrassment the lawyer, who by now regrets his surly attitude, is forced to admit, " 'The one [he cannot bring himself to identify the good man as a Samaritan] who showed him mercy.' " With amazing simplicity, and reserving judgment, Jesus says, " 'Go and do likewise.' " Then Jesus and his friends "went on their way" (10:38).[5]

Parables, Parables (Luke 10–14)

Skim through chapters 10 through 14 in the Gospel of Luke. How many parables do you count? You will probably see about twenty in these five chapters. As we near the center of Luke's Gospel, chapter 15, we encounter two parables that ask us if we have what it takes to be a student of Jesus; read Luke 14:25–33. Jesus' entourage now consists of twelve apostles, many disciples, and large crowds. In short order he will winnow this group down to size. Note his first statement: " 'Whoever comes to me and does not hate father and mother, wife and children, brothers and sisters, yes, and even life itself, cannot be my disciple.'" Whoa! "Hate" is a bit strong, no?[6] Jesus continues: "'Whoever does not carry the [the Greek text reads "his own" (or "her own")] cross and follow me cannot be my disciple.'" Jesus illustrates this with two parables on counting the cost of a project before making a full commitment. Jesus concludes: "'So therefore, none of you can become my disciple if you do not give up all your possessions.'" By now those in the crowd (and many of us) are not so sure about following this teacher.

Luke may be presenting a picture of Jesus that places him in the Hippocratic tradition. Many of us are familiar with the popularized version of the physicians' Hippocratic Oath—"Do no harm." However, the tradition is much deeper and richer than that. The literature coming from the school of Hippocrates spans seventy volumes and more than a century (400–325 BCE). The oath, which was a small but significant part of this tradition, represented a contract that bound a student to his teacher (often, but not always, a physician). In this oath the student promises to hold his teacher equal to his parents and to support the teacher financially—to give up everything. The student further promises to keep his life and learning pure and holy and to keep what is told to him by his patients a sacred secret never to be revealed. Is this the kind of contract Luke had in mind in this picture of Jesus? While Luke may or may not have been a physician, as a learned man he certainly would have known of this tradition. How many of the "large crowd" do you think signed this contract? How many disciples stayed on?[7] At least one of the twelve had his doubts.

Joy in Heaven (Luke 15:1–32)

At last we come to the center of Luke's Gospel. Luke, who is fond of doublets, now expands his examples to three so that you do not miss the point! In reading this Gospel one theme stands out above all others—God's joy. If you learn nothing else from this Gospel remember this: From the beginning of time God has been continually at work to celebrate God's own joy. Note how this stands in contrast to the grumbling[8] scribes and Pharisees: "'This fellow welcomes sinners and eats with them.'" So Jesus tells them a parable—actually three parables. Note the theme of each—finding that which is lost—and how each one ends—with a party. Also note the math involved with each story and how Jesus intensifies the theme as he moves from parable to parable.

Parable 1: A shepherd has lost one out of a hundred sheep (1 percent). He searches until he finds the wayward animal, and then calls his friends and neighbors over for a party: "'"Rejoice with me,"'" Jesus says. He then concludes: "'There will be more joy in heaven over one sinner who repents than over ninety-nine righteous persons who need no repentance'" (15:7).

Parable 2: A woman has lost one of her ten silver coins (10 percent). She searches until she finds it, and then calls her friends and neighbors over for a party. We understand that in the first parable Jesus was talking about God the Good Shepherd. Nothing new about that; read the Twenty-third Psalm. But is God a woman sweeping her house? Jesus has given traditional theology a significant twist. " ' "Rejoice with me, for I have found the coin that I had lost." ' " Again Jesus concludes, " 'There is joy in the presence of the angels of God over one sinner who repents.' "

Parable 3: Jesus begins his third parable bluntly: " 'There was a man who had two sons' " (15:11). He will lose one of them—50 percent!

I am writing this the day before Thanksgiving. Is there a more appropriate time to read the story of the Prodigal Son? Every year I remember my father greeting his twenty-something son as I entered his house many Thanksgivings ago. He laid a stiff hug on me and exclaimed, "Hooray! The prodigal has returned home!" He was genuinely glad to see me. And I was delighted to be inside his warm house full of Thanksgiving aromas and the usual assortment of relatives.

The Prodigal Son may be Jesus' best-loved parable. Who of us has not been on one end of that happy reunion? Who of us has not identified with one or more of the cast of characters in the story (except perhaps the fatted calf)? The story is elegantly simple. A son, the younger of two, wants his inheritance, and he wants it now to do with as he wishes. His father acquiesces. The son soon blows through his legacy only to find himself reduced to feeding pigs and sharing their slops. How low can you go? Even the servants in his father's house were better off than this. When he finally comes to his senses, he trudges home, fully (and rightly) expecting to be treated with contempt and disgust.

Surprise! There is not a hint of shame or rejection from his dad. Only a joyful, warm embrace followed by a welcome-home thanksgiving dinner. "Hooray! The prodigal has returned home!" This was not at all what the son was expecting. And not what his elder brother had in mind either. His jealousy speaks for itself, and his father does his best to mollify him. " ' "Son, you are always with me, and all that is mine is yours." ' " What more can you want? The father's final words bring down the curtain on this tale. They are words of Jesus that probably struck a responsive chord among those following him on the road, who would someday return to their own families. Words they might hope to hear from grateful, graceful parents: "Son. Daughter. Let's celebrate and rejoice! We had given you up for dead, but thank God you're alive! Let's eat!"

This parable is the gospel in a nutshell. From the beginning of time God has been continually at work to complete God's own joy. This joy can only be complete when every one of God's least, last, and lost children has returned to the kind, gracious, and patiently waiting parent.

Parables about Money: How Is Your 401(k)? (Luke 12:13–8; 14:7–14, 25–33; 16:1–13; 17:33)

You may have noticed by now that many of Jesus' parables deal with money—the business of life and the life of business. There was the story about the farmer who built larger and larger barns to hold more and more stuff (does this sound like your attic?). When he is finally ready to retire and enjoy his accumulated wealth, he dies (every recent retiree's worst nightmare; 12:13–21). " 'So it is with those who store up treasures for themselves but are not rich toward God' " (12:21). Note the other economic zingers at the end of Jesus' parables (also read the parable that leads up to the zinger).

- " 'Do not keep striving for what you are to eat and what you are to drink, and do not keep worrying . . . your Father knows that you need them. Instead, strive for [God's] kingdom, and these things will be given to you as well' " (12:29–31).

- " 'From everyone to whom much has been given, much will be required; and from the one to whom much has been entrusted, even more will be demanded' " (12:48).

- " 'When you give a banquet, invite the poor, the crippled, the lame, and the blind. And you will be blessed, because they cannot repay you, for you will be repaid at the resurrection of the righteous' " (14:13–14).

- " 'None of you can become my disciple if you do not give up all your possessions' " (14:33).

- " 'The children of this age are more shrewd in dealing with their own generation than are the children of light. And I tell you, make friends for yourselves by means of dishonest wealth so that when it is gone, they may welcome you into the eternal homes' " (16:8–9).

- " 'Those who try to make their life secure will lose it, but those who lose their life will keep it' " (17:33).

It would be difficult not to notice a theme here. Some of these sayings are enigmatic, especially 16:8–9. But remember, with parables there is no one right answer. Parables are an open invitation to enter into the spirit of the parable and learn something new about yourself and your relationship with God—and maybe even with those around you.

Jesus and Zacchaeus (19:1–10)

The last stop on Jesus' journey brings him to Jericho, which lies on a trade route about twenty-five miles east of Jerusalem. Traders moving goods in and out of Judea were required to stop at the border to pay a customs tax. This made Zacchaeus, a chief tax collector, a relatively wealthy man, "relatively" being the operative word. The social strata in Roman provincial society looked something like this (the percentages are rough approximations):

2–5 percent wealthy, ruling elite

10–20 percent landowners, high-level bureaucrats, army officers

40–50 percent service groups: peasants who lived hand-to-mouth existences as tenant farmers, craftsmen, and shopkeepers

15–20 percent slaves attached to households of the above three classes

15–20 percent day laborers working as farm hands, shepherds, apprentices, shop assistants

10–15 percent destitute beggars

As chief tax collector, Zacchaeus was well paid (probably in the second category above).[9] To the average peasant, he was rich. He was also short,[10] and he did the unthinkable. This man of substance acted like a child, climbing a sycamore tree—a tree with low-hanging, uncultivated figs that poor people ate. Even Jesus did the unthinkable by inviting himself to dine with Zacchaeus, claiming that it was the will of God: " 'I *must* stay at your house today' " (italics added). The Greek term translated as "must" (*dei*) carries much theological weight, and the reader encounters it often in Luke's Gospel. It is the same divine imperative Jesus used in the parable of the Prodigal Son in Luke 15—the father *must* celebrate the return of his son. Zacchaeus welcomes Jesus "joyfully" while the crowd grumbles. What was Jesus thinking?

The conversation between Jesus and Zacchaeus is fascinating. Zacchaeus begins by proclaiming his righteousness. To emphasize his point Zacchaeus stands up from the dinner table and says, "Look sir! Half of my possessions I give to the poor, and anyone I have overtaxed I reimburse fourfold" (au. trans.). Note the verbs "give" and "reimburse." In the Greek text these verbs are in the present tense. It is what Zacchaeus does in his everyday life. He goes beyond Roman and Jewish law in his dealings with others. Your English translation probably renders these as future-tense verbs,[11] suggesting that it is what Zacchaeus intends to do. What difference do these two ways of translating the verbs make? What do you think of Zacchaeus? What did Jesus think of Zacchaeus? Read on: " 'Today salvation has come to this house because even he is a son of Abraham.'" Jesus reminds the grumbling crowd that Zacchaeus is one of them. While he works for the Romans, he is also a righteous Jew. They may consider him a lost soul—a sinner. But Jesus reminds them, and us, that the Son of Man came to seek and to save the lost.

Note the themes that Luke has woven together in this last story before Jerusalem: joy, a banquet (lots of food), Jesus befriending a tax collector, the idea that salvation is available today, and the Son of Man seeking out the lost. Luke sums up his Gospel with this story, and now he is ready to bring Jesus to Jerusalem and the destiny that awaits him there.

Notes

1. Luke records thirty-eight parables of Jesus, of which twenty-seven are found in these ten chapters.
2. *The American Heritage Dictionary of the English Language* (New York: Dell Publishing Company, 1976), 515.
3. For example, see Ezek. 20:46; 25:2; 28:21; 29:2; 35:2; 38:2.
4. The word most often translated as "love" in our New Testament is from the Greek term *agapē*. The ethicist Joseph Fletcher rendered an excellent understanding of this word as "willing the good for the neighbor." It is not just a passive response; it is putting volition into action—doing something for the good of our neighbor.
5. One would think the lawyer might give up, but he didn't—which does not bode well for Jesus. Read 11:45–54.
6. Compare Matthew's lighter touch in 10:37–38.
7. Remember that Jesus functioned as a healer as well as a teacher. His own disciples eventually become healers and teachers in their own rights and in his name (see Luke's Acts of the Apostles).
8. The same unpleasant onomatopoetic term (*gogguzo*) is used in the Greek OT to describe the Israelites grumbling against Moses over their hardships in the wilderness.
9. See chap. 2, p. 20.
10. However, Luke's story is ambiguous. Who was short? Zacchaeus or Jesus? Let's assume Luke meant Zacchaeus.
11. Other modern translations follow suit. Why do you think translators offer this translation?

Chapter Five

Jesus in Jerusalem

A Study of Luke 19:28–22:38

Jesus Enters Jerusalem (19:28–48)

The reader knows that we are nearing the end of Luke's story about Jesus. Luke has brought us an "orderly account" of Jesus' life, beginning with his birth and lineage, continuing with his work as a healer in Galilee and as a teacher while walking from Galilee to Judea, and finally bringing Jesus to Jerusalem, which Pharisees thought of as the "center of the navel of the universe" (Romans might have disagreed). Here Jesus will have one last opportunity to teach about the kingdom of God, have one last unforgettable meal with his disciples, say a final prayer, and exhale his last breath. We know the end of Luke's story. Let's look closely at some of his narrative that carries us to that end.

Jesus had his entry into Jerusalem well orchestrated. He sent two disciples ahead to retrieve a "colt." Luke, unlike Matthew, does not specify the kind of colt—donkey or horse? What difference might this make? Jesus will ride the animal from the Mount of Olives overlooking Jerusalem, down into and across the Kidron Valley, up to the city gates, and into Jerusalem.

The story of Jesus' entry into Jerusalem is familiar to us. It is so familiar that we can overlook the obvious. Christians are accustomed to celebrate this day as "Palm Sunday."[1] But where are the palms? Instead of having them wave palm fronds, which would mark the entrance of a conquering hero (as in the other Gospels), Luke presents people throwing off their outer garments and spreading them on the ground in front of the animal bearing Jesus. They have divested themselves of symbols of status and allow the animal to trample on them. Luke continues his description:

> The whole multitude of the disciples began to praise God joyfully with a loud voice for all the deeds of power they had seen, saying,
>
> > "Blessed is the king
> > who comes in the name of the Lord!
> > Peace in heaven,
> > and glory in the highest heaven!" (19:37–38)

If this sounds familiar, it should. Reread the doxology the angels sang at Jesus' birth (2:14). You might want to compare the cheer of the crowd in all four Gospels. Note that Mark and Matthew simply say that Jesus is "the one" who comes in the name of the Lord (Mark 11:9; Matt. 21:9). Luke and John are more specific, identifying Jesus as "the king" who comes in the name of the Lord (Luke 19:38; John 12:13).

By now you may be confused by Luke's account of Jesus' entry into Jerusalem (it was probably confusing also for his first readers). First, Luke is ambiguous about the mode of Jesus' transportation—horse (hero) or donkey (low status)? Second, there is no palm waving but garment dropping instead. Third, Jesus is hailed as king, not just "the one." We may be confused, but onlookers were not. Some of the Pharisees in the crowd shout with alarm, "'Teacher! Order your disciples to stop!'" (19:39). Why might Pharisees be anxious about this scene?

Now read the words of Jesus as he weeps over Jerusalem (19:42–44). His prediction describes what happened thirty-five years later when the Roman army laid siege to Jerusalem to clear the city of anti-Roman zealots. This reminds us that Luke was a fine first-century historian. It looks as if Luke has recast the events of 65–70 CE into this scene (also read Luke's version of the "Synoptic Apocalypse" in 21:20–24).

Jesus' first action in Jerusalem was to enter the temple, the most sacred place on earth for first-century Jews. This is *the* place to worship the God of Israel. One would expect Jesus to go there to pray. But no. He went there to disturb the peace (to put it mildly). Perhaps he went to pray; he quoted the prophet Isaiah's lofty thoughts about this sacred space: "My house shall be called a house of prayer" (Isa. 56:7). But what he found was "a den of robbers," this time quoting Jeremiah (Jer. 7:11). High expectation turned into empty frustration and ended in furious action. "He began to drive out those who were selling things there," and he began teaching every day in the temple. Reaction against Jesus had spread dangerously beyond the Pharisees. Now "the chief priests [who managed the temple], scribes [the only authorized teachers in the temple], and the leaders of the people kept looking for a way to kill him" (19:47).

Jesus Resumes Teaching in the Temple (20:1–21:38)

The first thing to note about this section is what Jesus does. He teaches. The second thing to note is where he is—at the social and religious heart of first-century Judaism. Like any good religious and political reformer, if Jesus is to make a difference he must take his message to the center of religious and political power (even as Martin Luther visited Rome or Martin Luther King Jr. led the march on Washington). The third thing to note is the shift in those who oppose Jesus. While he was traveling about in Galilee, his opposition came mainly from Pharisees, whose authority was localized in each community synagogue. In Jerusalem their authority was greatly overshadowed by those in charge of the temple: the Sadducees, chief priests, and the scribes who served them. These "leaders of the people," who long ago made peace with their Roman overlords, were a much more formidable foe. Nevertheless Jesus was undaunted.

The leaders first challenge Jesus about the source of *his* authority. Who is he to challenge their authority (20:1–7)? Jesus neatly sidesteps their question and follows it with a parable (20:9–18). Read this parable and consider a few things along the way. Who might the figures in the parable represent? The vineyard owner? The owner's slaves? The owner's "beloved son"? The tenants? We could hear this parable on two different levels, two different time frames, and two different perspectives

For Jesus' hearers (~30 CE) the owner may or may not be God. Peasants were accustomed to absentee landlords and tenant farming, where rents and taxes often took most of their income, leaving them with barely enough to live on. Those hearing Jesus tell this story would probably identify with the tenants. They might conclude that the tenants were right; they should just take the land and claim its benefits for themselves. But Jesus concludes that the landlord sent his slaves and finally his own son to rightly collect what was due.

For Luke's hearers (~85 CE) the parable shifts a bit. For those in the early Christian community the owner can be identified as God, the slaves were the prophets, and the beloved son was Jesus. Moreover, Luke probably assumed a level of biblical literacy that prompted his hearers to remember Isaiah's parable of the vineyard (Isa. 5:1–13; be sure to read this parable). In Isaiah's story[2] God had planted a beautiful vineyard (God's own people—"inhabitants of Jerusalem and people of Judah") that yielded only sour grapes.

In a prophetic move not unlike Isaiah's, Jesus says that the owner "will come and destroy those tenants and give the vineyard to others" (20:16). What did Jesus mean by this? Would God give up on Israel and give her land to others? The peasants who heard Jesus could only respond, "Heaven forbid!" The leaders of the people, the chief priests and scribes, harbored much deeper foreboding. They wanted an end to this kind of teaching, "so they watched him" (20:20).

The next short scene in Luke's Gospel (20:20–26) brings us to the heart of the political problem for Judean Jews of the first century. Spies are sent by the temple leaders to ask Jesus one simple question, prefaced by one of the most disingenuous remarks in the whole Bible: "'Teacher, we know that you are right in what you say and teach, and you show deference to no one, but teach the way of God in accordance with truth'" (20:21). Their question takes half as many words. "'Is is lawful for us to pay taxes to the emperor, or not?'" Jesus is not about to stumble over this query. He asks for his interrogators to show him a coin: "'Whose head and whose title does it bear?'" They had produced a Roman denarius that was engraved with the image of Emperor Tiberius, and the inscription read, "Tiberius Caesar, Augustus, Son of Divine Augustus," a violation of the first two commandments given by God to Israel. In effect Jesus says, "Since you choose to engage in idolatry in order to receive the benefits of the empire, then by all means pay the emperor his due. End of discussion." It is worth noting that there was another currency the spies could have pulled from their pockets—the temple shekel, which would bear neither a human image nor a reference to a divine being other than the God of Israel.[3]

✓ Jesus' Last Speech (21:1–38)

Chapter 21 of Luke's Gospel is devoted to Jesus' teaching about the end times. Luke begins by describing what Jesus and his followers see as they approach the temple. They see a magnificent building "adorned with beautiful stones and gifts dedicated to God" (21:5). Herod the Great had rebuilt the temple as much a monument to himself as to God. He spared no expense, using the finest Roman architects, contractors, and materials. It was absolutely beautiful. Jesus, however, zeros in on another aspect of temple life. Having observed the wealthy put their gifts in the collection box, Jesus watches a woman deposit two of the smallest coins in circulation—two pennies. Jesus offers his final comment on current economics, and it deserves repeating: "'Truly I tell you, this poor widow has put in more than all of them; for all of them have contributed out of their abundance, but she out of her poverty has put in all she had to live on'" (21:3–4).

Read this chapter carefully. Jesus teaches about "the end," but the end of what? Some might read this chapter as signifying an apocalyptic end of the world as we know it. Jesus does speak about cosmic signs and earthly distress, people fainting from fear and foreboding, and the Son of Man coming from heaven in a cloud. One could also read this chapter historically. There will be wars and insurrections, famines and plagues, arrests and persecutions, betrayal and martyrdom. Finally, says Jesus, " 'When you see Jerusalem surrounded by armies, then know that its desolation has come near' " (21:20). This certainly sounds like events leading up to the siege and destruction of Jerusalem by the Roman legions in 70 CE. Jesus continues: " 'Then those in Judea must flee to the mountains [as did Jerusalem Christians just prior to the final Roman siege], . . . and those out in the country must not enter it [good advice].' " Jesus then offers an interesting comment: " 'For these are days of vengeance.' " Revenge for what? Think about that one. Christians of the second and third centuries arrived at an uncomfortable conclusion about this. Jesus continues: " 'For there will be great distress on the earth and wrath against this people [whom did Jesus/Luke have in mind?]; they will fall by the edge of the sword and be taken away as captives among all nations; and Jerusalem will be trampled on by the Gentiles, until the times of the Gentiles are fulfilled" (21:23–24, italics added). This is what happened during the Jewish-Roman war, and it sounds a bit like Luke (85 CE) has inserted events (70 CE) into this prophecy of Jesus (30 CE). What do you think? Has Luke historicized Jesus' apocalyptic teaching?[4]

Jesus finishes his apocalyptic lesson by asking his followers to be on guard and stay alert, " 'praying that you may have the strength to escape all these things that will take place, and to stand before the Son of Man' " (21:36). His disciples are to prepare for events that Luke knows will inevitably happen.

The (Almost) Last Supper (22:1–38)

In a few terse sentences Luke introduces the reader to the meal we know as "The Last Supper," though Jesus will eat two more times with his disciples (24:28–31, 36–43). Luke tells us that Jesus will celebrate the Feast of Unleavened Bread, or Passover. It was a major celebration in the Jewish community of God's liberation of the Hebrews, who were slaves in Egypt, from their overlords (about 1250 BCE).[5] The Hebrews, having been warned that the angel of death was descending on Egypt to slay the firstborn of each household, were instructed to smear the blood of a lamb on the doorposts of their houses. The angel of death would "pass over" these houses. The Egyptians were not in on the secret, so after a night of sheer terror they implored the Hebrew slaves to leave, which of course they did.

Now let's look carefully at Luke's introduction to this scene (22:1–6). Luke reiterates that serious trouble lies ahead for Jesus not only from the temple hierarchy but from Satan himself. Some scholars have noted that Luke presents the time of Jesus' earthly ministry as one free of Satanic interference. At the end of

Jesus' forty-day test before the beginning of his work Luke reports that the devil "departed from him until an opportune time" (4:13). This is that "opportune time" as Satan enters into one of Jesus' own followers, Judas, who will betray him to the temple authorities.

The disciples, led by Peter and John, rented a large guest room for their celebration, ordered the food, and set the table. When everything was ready, Jesus entered and took his place at the table. After his opening remarks (read 22:15), he lifted a cup of wine and offered an odd toast in which he said that this would be his last sip of wine " 'until the kingdom of God comes.' " Luke continues:

> Then he took a loaf of bread, and when he had given thanks, he broke it and gave it to them, saying, "This is my body, which is given for you. Do this in remembrance of me." And he did the same with the cup after supper, saying, "This cup that is poured out for you is the new covenant in my blood." (22:19–20)

Do you find anything odd about the sequence of bread and wine in this "Last Supper"? How is Communion celebrated at your church? Early Christian scribes struggled with this text. Some early manuscripts do not contain the words " 'This is my body . . . the new covenant in my blood' " (vv. 19b–20). It may be that in Luke's community Communion was celebrated by offering wine first and then bread, and this may reflect ambiguity about this celebration in the early church.[6] Later scribes may have tried to correct Luke's order of things by inserting verses 19b–20.

The heart of this meal is the sharing of bread, the staple of life. Note the formula that Luke uses to describe Jesus' action (verse 19): when he had given thanks for the bread, he broke it, and he gave it. It is a formula we have already seen in the feeding of the five thousand (9:10–17), and we shall see it again in his final meal with two disciples on the Emmaus road (24:30). Luke, like the other Gospel writers, emphasizes this point through repetition. It is *the* important aspect of a disciple's life with Jesus. Luke reminds us over and over again about the central importance of a common meal (Communion) that Jesus wishes to share with all of his disciples of every time and place, including Judas and Peter, you and me. The bread is a prophetic symbol of his own body that he blesses, breaks, and gives to all of his disciples—faithful and unfaithful alike.

Like some dinners with close friends the conversation occasionally turns testy. The disciples argue about which of them is Jesus' best friend. Who is the greatest? Who deserves the best seat at the table, close to the teacher? This social situation would customarily demand a pecking order.[7] The most seasoned students (Peter, James, and John) could claim places of honor close to the teacher while neophytes sat at a distance. As usual, Jesus' response reverses expectations: " 'The greatest among you must become like the youngest, and the leader like one who serves. . . . I am among you as one who serves.' " Yes, you will have places of honor, Jesus tells his disciples, but not now. First Satan will " 'sift all of you like wheat.' " Jesus knows that in short order his disciples will abandon him (Mark emphasizes this point; 14:27, 50). Nevertheless he has prayed that they might remain faithful and eventually strengthen weaker brothers and sisters (Luke has given his reader a preview of his second volume, the Acts of the Apostles).

Jesus' Final Instruction to His Disciples (22:35–38)

Jesus' final instruction to his disciples (22:35–38) seems strange—that the disciple who has no sword must sell his cloak to buy one. The disciples respond, " 'Lord, look, here are two swords.' "[8] Jesus says, " 'It is enough.' " What do you make of his request and their response? Now jump to verses 49–51 when one of Jesus' followers uses his sword against a slave of the high priest. Again Jesus says, " 'No more of this!' " This brings the reader to Jesus' arrest, trial, and execution.

Notes

1. Even my study Bible, *The New Oxford Annotated Bible*, titles this portion of Luke's Gospel as "Palm Sunday."
2. Actually it is a love song that Isaiah turns into a dirge.
3. And now we know the role of the money changers in the temple, who made their living by charging a premium for exchanging Roman denarii for temple shekels; only the latter currency could be used in purchasing animals for sacrifice.
4. You might want to compare Luke 21 and Mark 13 (Luke's source).
5. Exodus 12 records this event.
6. The *Didache* ("The Teaching of the Twelve Apostles") is an early second-century manual of church discipline that retains Luke's order: wine then bread (*Did.* 9.1–5).
7. Such was the case in the first-century Jewish community at Qumran (home of the Dead Sea Scrolls).
8. Did each disciple have two swords?

Chapter Six

The Arrest, Trial, and Death of Jesus

A Study of Luke 22:39–23:56

Jesus' Arrest and Peter's Denial (22:39–62)

So far Luke's story of Jesus has proceeded at a brisk pace—the birth of Jesus took place in Judea (Luke 1–2), his early ministry was in Galilee (Luke 3–9), he traveled south to Judea teaching along the way (Luke 9–19), and he taught for a week in Jerusalem (Luke 19–22). Now Luke slows the pace of his narration almost to an hour-by-hour crawl (Luke 23–24).

Luke tells us that it was Jesus' custom to spend his evenings on the Mount of Olives, a beautiful garden that offered a wonderful view of Jerusalem (21:37). After his final meal Jesus went to the garden one last time to pray and to instruct his disciples to pray as well.

Luke's particular portrait of Jesus emerges clearly in this scene. Compare the description of Jesus offered by Luke and his source, the Gospel of Mark (Mark 14:32–42; Luke 22:40–46). In Mark Jesus is "distressed and agitated . . . 'deeply grieved, even to death.'" He throws himself on the ground and prays that "the hour might pass from him" (14:33–35). Luke, by contrast, has Jesus simply kneel down to offer a short prayer, " 'Father, if you are willing, remove this cup from me; yet, not my will but yours be done' " (22:42). The next two verses in Luke's Gospel are a bit of a mystery. They are probably set in brackets in your version of the Gospel, which means that the translators of Luke's Gospel had questions about their place in the text. Some of the earliest manuscripts of Luke's Gospel do not contain these words. It may be that some later scribe, intent on making Luke consistent with Mark (and Matthew), made this descriptive insertion. It can also be argued that Luke is not emphasizing Jesus' anxiety (as in Mark) but his perseverance in aligning himself with God's will no matter what. The terms "strength," "anguish," and "sweat . . . like blood" are terms drawn from the realm of athletics. Jesus is readying himself for his final contest and victory. Unlike in Mark's Gospel, Luke's Jesus does not grieve. Luke shifts that emotion onto the disciples (22:45), and Jesus attempts to alleviate it by reiterating his instruction " 'Pray that you may not come into the time of trial' " (22:40, 46).

The arrest of Jesus by the temple police takes place quickly, though not without incident. Luke notes that one of the disciples asks, " 'Lord, should we strike with the sword?' " Before Jesus has a chance to answer, one of his followers cut off the *right* ear of a slave of the high priest. The right ear is a tiny detail that is a perfect example of how a story expands with time. Consider Mark (~65 CE), Luke (~85 CE), and John (~100 CE). Mark notes that an ear of the slave had been cut off (14:47). Luke adds that it was the slave's right ear and Jesus "healed him" (22:50–51). John adds even more detail: it was Simon Peter who cut off the slave's right ear; furthermore the slave's name was Malchus (18:10).

At this point it might be helpful to have Mark's Gospel available, for from time to time we will compare Mark and Luke as we read through the trial of Jesus.[1] Occasionally we will note when Luke diverges from his source (Mark) and ponder why.

When the brief skirmish is over, Jesus is taken captive and brought to the high priest's house for questioning. At this point Luke inserts the story of Peter's denial (three times) that he had been a disciple of Jesus. An interesting detail comes at the end of this episode. Luke notes that "Peter remembered the word of the Lord . . . , 'you will deny me three times' " (22:61). As we near the end of Luke's Gospel, the term "remember" (and related words) are frequently used. Memory of these events is critical to Luke (as well as to the other Gospel writers). Has your own memory been sharpened by particular events? Where were you when President Kennedy was assassinated? When the space shuttle Columbia exploded? When the Twin Towers came crashing down? When your father or mother died? For the earliest Christian community the same question was asked. Where were you when Jesus was crucified? The old African American spiritual captures the feeling exquisitely: "Were you there when they crucified my Lord?" Peter remembered, and it was Peter's memory that formed the core of this story.[2]

A second detail in this episode is located in the "word of the Lord" that Peter remembered. "'You will deny me *three times*'" (italics added). Early Christians might have known him as "Three-Times Peter." As you read through the Gospels and Acts, note how often the number three is associated with Peter. Peter denied Jesus three times. Peter was instructed three times by Jesus to "'feed my sheep'" (John 21:15–17). In a trance state, Peter was instructed three times by a voice from heaven to eat everything that was set before him, clean and unclean things alike (Acts 10:9–16). And finally Peter was instructed three times by an angel of the Lord to get up and leave the confinement of a prison cell (Acts 12:6–11).[3] Was Peter especially dense, consistently doubtful, obsessively careful, or simply reluctant to accept the fact that God had an important mission for him, a peasant fisherman? Whatever his motivations, he also had a conscience. "He went out and wept bitterly" (22:62). With that, Luke brings this scene to a close.

Interrogation (22:63–71)

After his arrest Jesus is taken to the high priest's house, where he is blindfolded, beaten, and mocked. When dawn finally arrives, he is brought before a council of elders, chief priests, and scribes for questioning. At this point it would be useful to have Mark's version of this scene before you.

Note first of all what Luke omits. Mark indicates that witnesses were brought in to testify against Jesus, but "many gave false testimony against him." Some had testified that Jesus had claimed that he would "destroy this temple, ... but even on this point their testimony did not agree" (Mark 14:56–59). This hearing involved such serious charges that it required at least two witnesses whose testimony would agree. Luke has omitted any reference to witnesses. It appears that he sought to eliminate any semblance of legitimacy to this hearing and to the charges that would result from it.

Second, read the all-important question put to Jesus by the high priest (Mark 14:61), and then read Luke's version of the question (22:67, 70). Notice the way Luke has split the original question into two parts. What difference might this make? Let's look at this in detail as follows (italics added):

Mark 14:61–62	Luke 22:67–70
Again the high priest asked him, "Are you *the Messiah,* the Son of the Blessed One?"	They said, "If you are *the Messiah,* tell us." He replied, "If I tell you, you will not believe; and if I question you, you will not answer. But from now on the Son of Man will be seated at the right hand of the power of God." All of them asked, "Are you, then, the Son of God?"
Jesus said, "I am; and 'you will see the Son of Man seated at the right hand of the Power,' and 'coming with the clouds of heaven.'".	[Jesus] said to them, "You say that I am."

It comes as no surprise that in Mark's Gospel the high priest roars his disapproval at Jesus' apparently antimonotheistic response, and the council condemns Jesus to death.

Now let's look at the exchange in Luke's Gospel. What do you make of Jesus' response to the question about being the Messiah? Is he direct? Indirect? Evasive? Obscure? Is he the Messiah? Maybe yes. Maybe no. Now read Jesus' response to the question about being the son of God (in the original Greek text "son" would not have been capitalized). "'You say that I am.'" This can also be translated, "You *may* say that I am," as if Jesus were giving permission for them to describe him in this way. Is this not therefore blasphemy? To Luke and his readers the answer was probably no. We are all sons and daughters of God. For Luke the more problematic charge against Jesus was the claim to be the Messiah, a king. There was only one king in the Roman Empire—Emperor Tiberius. Jesus (Luke's Jesus) is evasive about this claim. Luke also knows that a charge of being a child of God would hold little weight in a Roman courtroom—the next stop for the case against Jesus.

Jesus on Trial before Pontius Pilate (23:1–5)

Pontius Pilate was the Roman prefect of Judea, who reported to the Roman legate of Syria, who reported to the emperor in Rome. He held his office for an extraordinarily long time (26–36 CE), which might mean that he did a very good job or that he was exceedingly disliked by his superiors in Rome (Judea was an unruly backwater in the Roman Empire and an undesirable posting). He had a reputation as a tough administrator who would without hesitation resort to bloodshed in resolving conflicts with local malcontents. Jesus would not likely fare well in his court.

The first order of business was to establish the charge against Jesus. His accusers claim, "'We found this man perverting our nation, forbidding us to pay taxes to the emperor, and saying that he himself is the Messiah, a king.'" The last charge is the most emphatic. In case Pilate was not familiar with the Jewish term "Messiah" (a Hebrew word), they offer a Greek translation that Pilate would clearly understand—"a king!" Let's take a brief look at each of these serious charges: Yes, it was a crime under Roman law to lead a nation astray. And yet when it came to upholding Mosaic law, Jesus had been found blameless by the scribes and lawyers (10:25–28; 20:39). Rather than forbidding folks to pay taxes to Caesar, Jesus had clearly said, "'Render unto Caesar . . .'" (20:25). Finally, recall Jesus' circumvention of the charge against him: "Tell us if you are the Messiah" (22:67).

The charges brought against Jesus are specious and untrue. Pilate focused on the last and most serious charge: "'Are you the king of the Jews?'" This was a charge of *lese majesty*, lessening the majesty of the emperor. It indicated a direct challenge to the imperial authority and amounted to treason. Once again Jesus' answer was evasive:[4] "'You say so.'" Surprisingly, without any cross-examination Pilate declared Jesus to be innocent. The chief priests came back to their first charge: "'He stirs up the people.'" Pilate had been known to crush rebellions against Rome. Perhaps this would change his mind. Instead, Pilate heard the term "Galilee" and found a convenient way to get rid of this annoying case. He would ship Jesus off to Herod, the Roman tetrarch of Galilee.

Jesus and Herod (23:6–12)

There are several "Herods" that populate Luke's two volumes.[5] This Herod is Herod Antipas, the son of Herod the Great (see chapter 2). Like Pilate, Herod held the reins of power for a very long time (4 BCE to 39 CE). And like his father, he guarded his authority with ruthless power. He was apparently unconcerned about the politics of Jesus. He was, however, curious about Jesus' ability to perform miracles (think about the scene in *Jesus Christ Superstar* where Herod asks Jesus to "walk across my swimming pool"). Very little comes of this inquisition except that according to Luke it is another occasion for the mocking of Jesus (in Mark's Gospel the Roman soldiers do this). Unable to discover much to be concerned about, Herod returned him to Pilate. What do you make of Luke's footnote that Pilate and Herod became friends that very day?

Jesus and Pilate Again (23:13–38)

Pilate's patience with this case is wearing thin. Neither he nor Herod can find anything of substance to charge against Jesus. So he offers the pesky and persistent priests a compromise: "'I will therefore have him flogged and release him,'" which was the kind of beating meted out to local troublemakers.[6] Luke is emphatic that Pilate had found Jesus innocent of any serious charge and wanted to set him free. Luke finally brings the raucous scene to an end as the whipped-up crowd shouts for Jesus to be crucified—"and their voices prevailed."

Luke's presentation of these events, both the (so-called) trial and execution of Jesus, may be troubling to the careful Christian reader. In Mark's Gospel, Pilate also wanted "to satisfy the crowd . . . after flogging[7] Jesus, he handed him over to be crucified. Then the soldiers led him into the courtyard of the palace (that is, the governor's headquarters); and they called together the whole cohort" (15:15–16). Mark is very clear that Roman soldiers carried out the execution of Jesus.

Now consider Luke's version. After finding Jesus innocent three times, Pilate finally caved in and

> gave his verdict that *their* demand should be granted . . . and he handed Jesus over as *they* wished.
> As *they* led him away. . . .
> . . . . When *they* came to the place that is called The Skull, *they* crucified Jesus there. (23:24–26, 33, italics added)

Who are "*they*"?[8] Who exactly was responsible for Jesus' execution? Who did Luke want the reader to think killed Jesus? Has Luke subtly shifted responsibility off Roman shoulders?[9] If this is the case, then we might also wonder *why* Luke would do this. One might also wish to ponder the unintended consequences of Luke's presentation of the crucifixion of Jesus.

The Death of Jesus (23:39–56)

According to Luke, Jesus was crucified alongside two criminals. An inscription posted on the cross specified the charge against Jesus (23:38): "King of the Jews" is a charge of high treason, one of the few details about Jesus found in all four Gospels. Note that before he died Jesus had a final conversation with the two criminals. One of the criminals declared Jesus' innocence, to which Jesus responded, "'Today you will be with me in Paradise.'"

At about noon the sun turned dark, and a curtain of the temple was torn.[10] Immediately after this Jesus cried out with a loud voice: "'Father, into your hand I commend my spirit.'" Once again you might want to compare this relatively peaceful death to Mark's account, in which Jesus cried out to God, "'Why have you forsaken me?'" For Mark, Jesus died in agony as a suffering victim. For Luke, Jesus died in victory as a heroic martyr.

Following Jesus' death the reader finally encounters a genuine Roman soldier. We know this because his Roman rank is mentioned. He was a centurion. And once again compare his response to Jesus' death with the centurion in Mark's Gospel. Mark's centurion proclaims, "'Truly this man was God's Son!'"—a confession of faith.[11] Luke's centurion says, "'Certainly this man was innocent!'"—the final Roman judgment.

Ordinarily the bodies of executed criminals were dumped in a common grave. The body of Jesus, however, was treated with respect. It was handed over to a prominent member of the Jewish high council, Joseph of Arimathea, who wrapped the body of Jesus in a linen cloth and laid it in his own tomb. This took place on Friday afternoon. Luke tells the reader that those who followed Jesus to the bitter end—the women from Galilee (where are the male disciples?)—rested the whole next day. They remembered the Sabbath and kept it holy.[12]

Notes

1. Scholars have been doing this comparison for a long time. Contemporary students of the New Testament have been helped by a study aid called *Gospel Parallels* (Burton Throckmorton, ed. [Nashville: Thomas Nelson, 1992]), which arranges the three Synoptic Gospels (Matthew, Mark, and Luke; sometimes John is added) in parallel columns. This helps the reader see where Luke (and Matthew) has borrowed from Mark, what he modifies, and what he leaves out. Why would this matter?

2. The women who visited Jesus' tomb were instructed by two men in dazzling white clothes to remember the words of Jesus: "then they remembered his words" (24:6–8). The words "remember" and "tomb" are related in Greek, as they are in English. Cemeteries are sometimes called "Memorial Parks"—a special place to recall to memory a loved one who has died.

3. This scene is worth a look. It took Peter some time to realize he was not dreaming.

4. Jesus' answer might even have been insulting: "If you say so." However, Pilate did not receive it as an insult.

5. Herod the Great (king of the Jews at the time of Jesus' birth [Luke 1:5]), Herod Antipas (Herod's son [Luke 3:1; 9:7; 13:31–32; 23:7]), Herod Agrippa I (Herod's grandson [Acts 12:1]), and Herod Agrippa II (Herod's great-grandson [Acts 25:13]).

6. As happened to the apostle Paul on more than one occasion (2 Cor. 11:23).

7. The kind of furious, flesh-ripping beating that began the execution process. Luke has used a different Greek term.

8. Luke does mention soldiers at the foot of the cross (23:36). Whose soldiers are they? Luke had mentioned two types of "soldiers"—those belonging to the temple staff and those belonging to Herod. There has been no mention (yet) of explicitly Roman soldiers.

9. While this shift is subtle here, Luke is more explicit in his second volume (see Acts 2:23, 36; 3:13–15, 17).

10. It is impossible to know which of the thirteen curtains Luke had in mind. He may have simply copied his source.

11. It is interesting to speculate exactly what Mark's centurion might have meant. Remember that the Gospels were intended to be read aloud to an audience, with particular attention paid to voice inflection. While we usually read the centurion's statement positively (a confession of faith), it could also be read as a derisive jeer—"Really? This was the Son of God?" Luke's centurion is less ambiguous.

12. Exod. 20:8.

Chapter Seven

Resurrection and Ascension

A Study of Luke 24:1–53

If you are familiar with the resurrection stories in the Gospels, you may have wondered why they are so numerous and so varied. It was probably the case that the resurrection of Jesus had such a seminal and powerful influence on Jesus' disciples that it simply could not be fully described in just one story. As stories about the resurrection evolved over the decades, each Christian community developed its own version that addressed the didactic, theological, and historical needs of that community. Luke's narrative was a version of the resurrection that gained ascendancy in his particular Christian community.

It is no coincidence that Luke inserted "repentance" into his resurrection narrative (24:47). Jesus' resurrection, however it happened,[1] was an experience so profound that it compelled the disciples to repent—that is, to change their minds (the meaning of the Greek term *metanoia*) about Jesus. It was this radical change of mind about the mission and message of Jesus that was at the heart of the formation of the earliest church. The resurrection challenged people to change their minds about Jesus. Some had dismissed Jesus as a deluded crucified sophist.[2] For Luke, however, Jesus' resurrection represented God's victory over injustice, sloth, betrayal, and death.

This last section of Luke's Gospel, like the birth narratives (Luke 1–2), is a self-contained unit. In it Luke presents three stories about Jesus' resurrection: (1) the women discover an empty tomb; (2) two disciples have supper with Jesus at an inn; and (3) Jesus appears to the rest of his disciples in Jerusalem. An interesting thing to note about Luke's presentation is that he does not describe the resurrection itself—Jesus is not portrayed as walking out of the tomb. Rather, he narrates two kinds of stories: the discovery of the empty tomb and Jesus' postresurrection appearance to his disciples.

An Idle Tale (24:1–12)

Luke continues his slow and steady pace. The entire last chapter of his Gospel is devoted to a single day, the day we call Easter Sunday. He begins, "On the first day of the week," which is our Sunday, and then tells us that the women who had followed Jesus from Galilee have come to the tomb to complete the burial process for Jesus' body. To their surprise the large round stone (probably set into a groove in the ground) had already been rolled aside from the entrance to the tomb. There is no need for male disciples after all. "*Suddenly* two men in dazzling clothes" appear to them (italics added). Once again you might want to compare this with Luke's source. In Mark there is just one "young man dressed in a white robe" (Mark 16:5). Luke is not simply embellishing his source. These details (two men, dazzling clothes) suggest that Luke was thinking theologically. He is pointing the reader backward and forward. First, let's rewind Luke's story of Jesus back to the transfiguration (9:28–36). Jesus took Peter, James, and John up a mountain to pray. While Jesus was praying, his appearance changed, and his clothes "became dazzling white. *Suddenly* they saw two men. . . " (9:29–30, italics added). Luke further identifies these two men as Moses and Elijah, representing the Law and the Prophets. Luke continues, "They appeared in glory [this is a scene of divine transcendence] and were speaking of his departure [resurrection? ascension?], which he was about to accomplish at Jerusalem" (9:31).

Now flash forward to Luke's second volume, the Acts of the Apostles. In Acts 1:9–10, Jesus is ascending into heaven. While the disciples are looking up, "*suddenly*[3] two men in white robes stood by them" (italics added). Sound familiar? "They said, 'Men of Galilee, why do you stand looking up toward heaven? This Jesus, who has been taken up from you into heaven, will come in the same way as you saw him go into heaven'" (1:11). Luke does not mention this, but his readers would have identified the two men as Moses and Elijah, two biblical figures who had already ascended to heaven and have returned to accompany Jesus into the heavenly realm.

By now the pattern and theological message is clear. God has intervened in this tragic situation, turning defeat into victory. The men (Moses and Elijah) are his messengers. Their message to the women is simple and profound: " 'Why do you look for the living among the dead? . . . *Remember* how he told you. . . .' " (Luke 24:5–6, italics added here and in following passages). Remember the importance of remembering (see above, p. 51). The women at the *tomb* (*mnēma*) are instructed, " '*Remember* [*mnēmoneuō*] how he told you, while he was still in Galilee, that the Son of Man must be handed over to sinners, and be crucified, and on the third day rise again.' Then they *remembered* his words, and returning from the *tomb,* they told all this to the eleven and to all the rest" (24:6–9). Luke had a field day with this wordplay. We have the same play on words in English. Some cemeteries go by the name "Memorial Park"—literally a special place "to bring to memory" a loved one who has died.

This scene is so important to Luke that he identifies each of the women by name: Mary Magdalene, Joanna, Mary the mother of James (and Jesus; James is the next-oldest living son of Mary [he becomes an important figure in Luke's second volume]). They had experienced a theophany. Now, that's a big theological word that means they had a profound experience of the divine realm breaking into their humble and humiliating historical circumstance. Their reaction was as one might expect. They were both terrified and excited to tell the apostles what they had witnessed. When they relate their experience to the apostles, the reaction of the men is unexpected. Luke described the disciples as clueless: "But these words seemed to them an idle tale, and they did not believe them." Our earliest manuscripts of the New Testament conclude the scene here. Later scribes try to rehabilitate Peter, who ran to the tomb in order to validate the women's story.[4]

One Last Story (24:13–35)

By now we hope it is apparent to you that Luke is one of the best storytellers in the Bible. He has given us scenes (the Good Samaritan), phrases ("fatted calf"), and characters (Zacchaeus) that stick with the reader. His stories prod the mind, stimulate the imagination, and stir the heart. But like any author worth his salt, he has saved the best for last.

Now read through the story of the two disciples who encounter a stranger on the road to Emmaus, and reflect on it. Notice especially how emotions propel this story along. When you have finished reading, recount some of the details of this story. Enjoy!

- Two travelers,[5] walking on the road toward Emmaus,[6] discuss what had taken place in Jerusalem two days ago.

- They are joined by a stranger. The reader knows the stranger is Jesus, though "their eyes were kept from recognizing him."[7]

- The travelers were "looking sad."

- Jesus elicits their account of recent events in Jerusalem by feigning ignorance.

- Their grief descends to mockery toward their traveling companion: " 'Are you the *only* stranger in Jerusalem who does not know the things that have taken place there in these days?' "

- Continuing his charade the stranger asks, " 'What things?' "

- After recounting the death of Jesus, they speak of their dashed hope—" 'that [Jesus] was the one to redeem Israel.' "[8]

- They continue, " 'Some women of our group astounded us' " by reporting their discovery of an empty tomb, but no Jesus.

- The stranger now chides them for being " 'foolish' " and " 'slow of heart.' " In first-century human physiology the "heart," in both Greek and Hebrew texts, has the capacity for both thought and emotion. "Slow of heart" may be a polite way of saying "not too bright."

- As they walk along the road, the stranger offers his companions a crash course about the Messiah: "Beginning with Moses and all the prophets, he interpreted to them the things about himself in all the scriptures."

- As darkness descends, the travelers urge the stranger to join them for dinner at a local inn.[9]

- When they are at the table, the stranger "took bread, blessed and broke it, and gave it to them." Does this formula sound familiar?

- After the meal, "their eyes *were opened* [note the divine passive; see n. 7] and they recognized him; and he vanished from their sight" (italics added).

- After Jesus left they reflected on their experience. " 'Were not our hearts burning within us [as he taught them a new way to understand Scripture]' "?

- In spite of the darkness, "they got up and returned to Jerusalem" to tell the disciples "what had happened on the road, and how he had *been made known* [the divine passive once again; see n. 7] to them in the breaking of the bread" (italics added).

This single story highlights many of the major themes we have encountered in Luke's Gospel. Let's begin with some obvious themes and move toward implied themes:

- The centrality of grief and joy in our lives (think about the father in the story of the lost son).

- The importance of remembering Jesus, the peripatetic teacher, who interprets Scripture in new ways.

- The importance of hospitality, even toward the stranger who chides you—you might learn something.

- The importance of being a good guest even when the hosts are "slow of heart"—they have the capacity to learn.

- The importance of eating together. Every meal is not just any meal. It is an opportunity to reveal a greater presence among the diners. And who knows, dining with strangers might turn out to be an eye-opening experience.

- Finally, if Jesus is made known in the eating of that special meal called the Lord's Supper, why do many churches have this meal so infrequently?

This story is one for the road.[10] It is a story of ordinary people who had experienced extraordinary grief. And in the depth of their depression God intervened in the everyday events of ordinary life in extraordinary ways. Jesus, who entered this phase of their lives as a stranger, was suddenly revealed to them as the resurrected Christ in a very ordinary act that we do every day: "He had been made known to them in the breaking of the bread" (24:35).

The End (24:36–53)

This is one of the most fascinating scenes in the New Testament. It can be divided into three sections: (1) Jesus appears in the flesh to his disciples; (2) Jesus commissions his disciples to be witnesses; and (3) Jesus ascends into heaven. Let us look at a few details in each section.

Jesus Appears to His Disciples

From out of nowhere Jesus stood among his disciples and said to them, " 'Peace be with you.' " Luke indicates that they were "terrified," the same word he used to describe the women at the tomb (24:5). Luke conveys to his readers that there is a distinction to be made between a ghostly apparition and a bodily presence. The resurrected Jesus is touchable and has flesh and bones.[11]

Perhaps the more significant issue for Luke, as it was for Matthew and John, is the interplay between belief and doubt.[12] Even after seeing the marks of Jesus' suffering, his disciples are still filled with a mixture of joy, doubt, and wonder. For Luke, doubt is a component of belief. To paraphrase Augustine, the path to mature faith sometimes leads through a forest of doubt. And finally, Jesus responded as he frequently did throughout Luke's Gospel: "Let's eat!"

Jesus Commissions His Disciples

As Luke brings his story to a close he reminds the reader of his major themes. One last time he presents Jesus as a teacher who "opened their minds to understand the scriptures."[13] Moreover, he encourages a particular way of interpreting Scripture—christologically. Finally, Jesus commissions his disciples: " 'You are witnesses of these things,' " and offers one last command: " 'Stay here in the city until you have been clothed with power from on high' " (vv. 48–49). The reader will need to read Luke's second volume to discover what that was about.

Luke's Grand Finale

We have come to the last few sentences of Luke's Gospel. Please read them carefully. You might also want to read a few verses from the opening of Luke's second volume, the Acts of the Apostles—especially Acts 1:3–9. You will note that Luke has Jesus ascend twice, and you might wonder why. Of course that is an impossible question to answer with any assurance, but it may simply be that Luke wished to round off his first volume. Luke's Gospel stands on its own as a complete story of Jesus, from incarnation to ascension. His second volume is a continuation of this story, the story of the first Christian community. Luke simply wanted to emphasize that Jesus "was carried [note again the divine-passive verb] into heaven" (v. 51). While he is no longer on earth physically, he is still with us as he was with those first disciples.

Now is the time to play the last movement of Beethoven's Ninth Symphony—the "Ode to Joy." Note the way Luke, the great literary artist, has punctuated the end of his story: *Worship! Joy! Thanksgiving!*

Epilogue: What Have We Learned from Luke's Story of Jesus?

In his preface Luke indicated that he was writing in order to instruct a disciple named Theophilus, literally "lover of God." Over the centuries countless lovers of God who wished to be good disciples of Jesus have learned much from Luke. And we contemporary lovers of God continue to learn how to be better disciples with each page of Luke's Gospel.

We have learned the importance of careful instruction by observing Jesus the model teacher. He taught using simple stories and aphorisms, inviting the hearer to enter his parables to consider how she or he relates to every being that inhabits this earth. He did not force his didactic agenda, but we got his point.

We learned to reach out to everyone in need—the least, the last, the lost. Jesus was the exemplary healer who touched the untouchable. He helped them see and hear and walk. He fed their spirits and bodies. His disciples continued his mission of compassion (see Luke's second volume).

Jesus helped us to discover that we are part of God's joyful embrace of the whole human species. The door to his community is open wide, and everyone is welcome inside. Basic human needs will be met. There is food for all in the messianic community—*koinonia Christou*. He calls his disciples to share their material resources generously and not to hold back. We do not possess anything. All that we have is a gift from God. In helping those in need we render to God (in whose image the other is made) the things that are God's.

We have discovered that Jesus welcomed the company of anyone who wished to walk along, men and women, poor and rich, young and old. This lack of concern about class or gender distinctions carried over to the early Christian community that Luke records in his second volume. The Acts of the Apostles describes the church as a model of unity *and* diversity, a new and exciting possibility for life in the Roman Empire.

One final note. As you may have noticed, Luke was a master of irony. Consider once again his preface. Luke addressed Theophilus as "most excellent," which denotes very high status in the Roman Empire. Given what Theophilus was instructed about Jesus' message about wealth, power, and status, we wonder what he might have learned from Luke's Gospel—and how he was changed.

How has Luke instructed you? How has Luke helped you become a more faithful disciple?

Notes

1. Luke indicates that Jesus emerged from the tomb as "flesh and bones" (24:39). For another point of view you might want to read Paul's description of the resurrected *spiritual* body in 1 Cor. 15 (written about thirty years

before Luke's Gospel), precisely what Luke says Jesus was not (24:37, 39; "ghost" = "spirit" in Greek).

2. See, for example, the Roman historian Tacitus, *Annals*, 15.44, and the satirist Lucian of Somasata, *The Death of Peregrinus*, 13.

3. Each time Luke introduces the two men, he uses the same term (*idou*), which can mean "suddenly" or "behold!" In doing this he wants to get the reader's attention. Wake up! Something important is about to happen.

4. Your Bible may have a footnote to this effect.

5. Who were they? They might have been a man and woman (Luke's usual pattern)—Mr. and Ms. Cleopas? They were probably disciples, but not part of "the twelve" (now eleven; see 24:33).

6. About seven miles east of Jerusalem.

7. Often a verb used in a passive voice ("their eyes *were kept*"), especially in a scene like this, indicates an action initiated by God—a "divine passive."

8. Did their hope have political undertones (see Acts 1:6)?

9. This scene provided the inspiration for the wonderful nineteenth-century hymn "Abide with me; fast falls the eventide."

10. Which, by the way (pun intended), was one of the early names claimed by the Christian community—the Road, the Way (Acts 9:2; 19:9, 23; 22:4; 24:14, 22).

11. Luke's resurrected Jesus is significantly different from John's description of Jesus, who instructs Mary Magdalene not to touch him " 'because I have not yet ascended to the Father' " (John 20:17).

12. See Matt. 28:17 and John 20:24–31.

13. This is one of the earliest references to the three-part canon of the Hebrew Bible—Moses (Torah), Prophets, Psalms (Writings).

Part Two

LEADER'S GUIDE

DONALD L. GRIGGS

Guidelines for Bible Study Leaders

Goals of the Course

Even though this course on the Gospel of Luke could be read and studied without being a member of a class, the greatest value of the study will be realized when the reader is engaged with others who are companions on the journey. As I prepared these session plans, I had in mind a number of goals that I hope the participants will experience as a result of their study. I hope that participants will

- bring to their study a desire to enter more deeply into the world of the Bible and the world of the Gospel of Luke.

- enjoy studying the Bible with others.

- come to a greater understanding and appreciation of the structure and message of the Gospel of Luke.

- share their insights, questions, and affirmations with other study participants.

- develop a discipline of reading and studying the Bible on a regular basis.

Basic Teaching Principles

As I prepared these session plans, I worked hard to implement a number of basic principles for effective teaching and leading. The foundational principle is an attempt to involve everyone in the class in as many activities as possible during every session every week. That's a big goal! You will see this principle present in all of the session plans that follow. I had at least a dozen other principles in mind as I designed this course:

- The leader serves best as companion and guide in the journey of the course.

- The leader provides sufficient information but not so much that participants lose the joy of discovery.

- Motivation for learning involves enjoying and completing tasks as well as making choices.

- Participants learn best when a variety of activities and resources are used in order to respond to their different interests, needs, and learning styles.

- Participants need to be invited to express their feelings, ideas, and beliefs in creative ways that are appropriate to them and to the subject matter.

- All participants need opportunities to share what they understand and believe.

- Open-ended questions invite interpretation, reflection, and application.

- Persons are nurtured in faith when they share their faith stories with one another.

- All teaching and learning happens in planned and unplanned ways and is for the purpose of increasing biblical literacy and faithful discipleship.

- The Bible becomes the living word of God when leaders and learners see their own faith stories expressed in Scripture.

- The Bible provides many resources to prompt our prayers, confessions of faith, and commitments to the ministry of Jesus Christ.

Room Arrangement

Arrange the room where you meet in such a way that participants are seated at tables. Tables are important because they provide space for all of the materials and the coffee cups. They also suggest that participants are going to work; they are not to just sit and listen to a lecture. If members of the group do not know everyone in the group, then they all need name tags. Set up a table with hot water and makings for coffee, tea, and hot chocolate just inside the entrance to the room so that everyone can get a cup and then find a seat. If you have a small group, arrange the tables in a rectangle or square so that everyone can see all the other members of the group. With a small group you will be able to be seated with them. If you have a large group, arrange the tables in a fan shape pointed toward the front so the participants can see the leader standing at the front of the group with a white board, newsprint easel, or bulletin board.

Resources

On the first week, be sure to provide Bibles for those who do not bring one. Continue to provide Bibles for those occasions when it is important for everyone to have the same translation and edition if you plan for them all to look at the same pages at the same time. However, encourage everyone to bring his or her own Bible. In addition to the Bibles, borrow from the church library, the pastor's library, and your own library copies of Bible dictionaries, Luke commentaries, and Bible atlases. A church library will not ordinarily have enough Bible dictionaries for each person to have one with which to work. For those sessions where members are responsible for searching for information about a passage, person, or event in Luke, make photocopies of the appropriate articles in a Bible dictionary, encyclopedia, or atlas. For one-time use, for one class, it is not a violation of the copyright laws.

Be sure to provide paper and pencils for those who don't bring them. Almost all of the activity sheets to be used by the participants are at the end of the respective session plans for which they will be used. There may be several other activity sheets that will need to be reproduced for the participants.

Time

I planned each session to be an hour in length. If you have less than an hour, you will have to make some adjustments. It will be better to leave an activity out than to rush class members through all of the planned activities. Perhaps it would be possible in your situation to schedule more than seven sessions. There is probably enough material here for ten or more sessions. If you have that much time, you will truly be able to deal with everything carefully without hurrying.

If you and your group have not already studied one of the first two books in this Bible study series, *The Bible from Scratch: The Old Testament for Beginners* or *The Bible from Scratch: The New Testament for Beginners,* you may find it helpful to use session 1 from either of those courses as an introduction to this style of Bible study.

Final Word

As you prepare to teach this course, it is essential that you read each chapter of part 1 as you consider your teaching strategy for each session of the course. You should assume that many, though not all, of the participants will have read the respective chapter before coming to the class session, and you should be as familiar with the material as they are. Exploring the Gospel of Luke with fellow pilgrims on the journey of faith will be for them and for you a challenging, inspiring, growing, and satisfying experience. May God bless you with many discoveries and much joy on this journey. If you and the members of your Bible study group find this course to be helpful, you may want to plan for the next course in the series, *Exodus from Scratch: The Old Testament for Beginners.*

Session One

Luke Says Hello
and Introduces Jesus

A Study of Luke 1:1–2:52

BEFORE THE SESSION
Focus of the Session

In this session we will get the course off to a good start by building community, focusing on some of the features of Luke's Gospel, reflecting on Mary's song of praise, and comparing Luke's narrative of Jesus' birth with the narrative of John the Baptist's birth.

Advance Preparation

- Take the time to read the whole of the Gospel of Luke. Try to do it in one sitting. This will help you gain a sense of the structure, flow, and key features of the Gospel.

- Read chapter 1 in the Participant's Guide (pp. 9–17).

- Read an introductory article or two about Luke in a study Bible or Bible dictionary.

- Gather several Bible study tools to share with the participants: a single-volume Bible commentary and a commentary on the Gospel of Luke, a Gospel parallels book if one is available, a Bible dictionary, and one or more study Bibles.

- Secure ahead of time a recording of the Magnificat to use in one of the planned activities. You will also need to arrange for a CD player or laptop computer with extended speakers in order to play the song so that all can hear.

- The suggested closing activity is to sing the first stanza of the Christmas carol "Hark! The Herald Angels Sing." If you want to sing more than one stanza, you may need to secure hymnals or print out the words on newsprint or a handout sheet.

- Provide a few extra Bibles for those who forget to bring one.

Physical Arrangements

Reread the section of "Guidelines for Bible Study Leaders" that offers suggestions regarding room arrangement, resources and materials, and refreshments. You should have everything ready for the first session so that you can make a good first impression, especially for those who are new to Bible study.

DURING THE SESSION
Welcoming the Participants

You will feel more relaxed and ready for leading the session if you set up the refreshments and have everything ready before the first persons arrive. If you expect a large group, it will be helpful to have assistance from another person or two to take care of all the set-up arrangements. Ask the participants to sign in and make name tags for themselves. Greet each one by name and with a warm welcome. Check to see who needs to borrow a Bible and give them one. Encourage everyone to bring a Bible next week. If any of the participants do not already have a copy of this course book, you should give them one so that they will have access to any of the references you will make to it during the session.

Introducing the Course

As you begin the session, there are several points you will want to emphasize:

- This first session will introduce participants to the Gospel of Luke and look more closely at chapters 1 and 2.

- The remaining six sessions will move sequentially through the Gospel.

- The session plans will not necessarily repeat what is in the Participant's Guide but will be based on that material and the related portions of Luke.

- It is expected that participants will read the relevant chapter in the Participant's Guide in preparation for each session.

- All participants should bring a Bible to class, preferably a study Bible if they have access to one.

- There will be some presentation by the leader in each session, but much of the time the leader will be guiding the class members through a series of activities designed to engage them with the key Scriptures and main ideas of each session.

- There are no "dumb questions." All questions are appropriate. Encourage the participants to ask questions of the leader and the group.

- Everyone's insights, ideas, and affirmations will be received and respected. It is important to feel free to express what is in one's mind and heart.

After you have finished your introduction to the session, invite participants to begin their journey through the Gospel of Luke by joining you in a brief prayer.

Opening Prayer

Introduce this activity by stating that in each session there will be an opening prayer that will be prompted by the text of the week's study of Luke's Gospel. In this session a primary focus is on the birth narrative in the first two chapters of Luke, in which there are several names by which Jesus is identified. Our litany prayer is prompted by those names. Direct the participants to page 79 of the

Leader's Guide. You take the lead, and the participants respond. After praying the litany, invite the participants to share any insights that have come to them through hearing quotes from Luke and praying in response to them.

Building Community among the Participants

In this first session it will be important to take a little time for participants to introduce themselves. Invite each person to share three things about himself or herself: name, a memory of an early experience in church as a child, or a favorite story about Jesus. Be sure to introduce yourself in this activity, perhaps even first in order to model what you have in mind. After all have introduced themselves, affirm the wonderful memories and favorite Jesus stories that were shared and emphasize that it is a great foundation on which to build for your study of the Gospel of Luke.

Introducing Luke's Gospel

Since most participants will probably not have read in preparation for this first session, it would be helpful to provide an overview of the key points made in the introduction to Luke in the Participant's Guide, pages 3 to 7. There are three possible ways you could summarize the main topics of the introduction. One way is for you to prepare a presentation to cover the key points. A second way is to direct the participants to the appropriate pages and "walk" them through the several sections by highlighting the key points in each. And a third way is to divide the class into several small groups and assign each group one of the sections. Provide time for them to read and to prepare a presentation of the key points of their section. If time is limited, you will want to choose one of the first two options since the third way will take more time.

Reflecting on Mary's Song of Praise

Writing about Mary's song of praise, the author of the Participant's Guide writes, "It is a hymn to God, the 'Savior,' who has looked with favor on the lowliness of his servant, Mary" (p. 12). Guide the participants through a process that helps them hear and reflect on this song of Mary that we know as the Magnificat.

- There are many musical renditions of the Magnificat from which you could choose to introduce this activity. You may have a recording in your collection, or you could borrow a CD from your public library, or you could download it from iTunes.

• First, lead your group to read in unison Luke 1:46–56.

• Then introduce your musical version of the prayer, and invite the participants to reflect on how the words and the music in this version express the meaning of the biblical text. Ask if anyone in the group has sung the Magnificat, and if so, invite them to share a few words about that experience.

• Present the song from a CD player or your laptop computer with external speakers.

• After listening to the Magnificat, guide the group in a brief time of reflection on their thoughts and feelings about how the music interprets the words of Scripture.

The author of the Participant's Guide writes, "It is difficult to miss the revolutionary nature (God is revolving the wheel of history) of Mary's song and Jesus' message" (p. 13). Take a few minutes to discuss several questions, such as those that follow or ones you have created.

• What do you see as "revolutionary" in Mary's song?

• How might Luke's audience have heard this theme?

• How might they have reacted to this message?

• What are some connections you see between Mary's song and what you know of Jesus' ministry that will be presented later in Luke's Gospel?

Comparing Two Birth Narratives

A unique feature of Luke's Gospel is the presentation of the narrative of Elizabeth's pregnancy and the birth of John. In this activity you will guide the group to compare the birth narratives of John and Jesus. Some suggested steps of the process are as follows:

• Turn to page 80 in the Leader's Guide, where you will find a worksheet to use in this activity.

• Divide the participants into groups of four. In each small group two persons will work with the John birth narrative and the other two with the Jesus narrative.

- Each pair reads its assigned passage and answers the questions.

- After the reading and discussion, invite the two pairs to share with each other what they have discovered in their birth narratives.

When the small groups have finished their work, gather back as a full group and spend a few minutes discussing several questions, such as those that follow or ones you have created.

- What are some contrasting differences between the two narratives?

- What are some striking similarities between the two narratives?

- In what ways do you see Luke setting the stage for what is to follow?

- What is most surprising to you in these birth narratives?

- The next time you see a nativity drama at Christmas in your church, how might this study influence what you will view and hear?

Closing

An appropriate way to close this session is to sing together the first stanza of the familiar Christmas carol "Hark! The Herald Angels Sing."

AFTER THE SESSION

Encourage the participants to read chapter 2 in the Participant's Guide and Luke 3:1–4:44 in preparation for the next class session.

A Litany Prompted by Names for Jesus

Leader: The angel said to Mary, "'You will conceive in your womb and bear a son, and you will name him Jesus'" (1:31).

Group: Revealing God, we thank and praise you for the gift of yourself in the birth of Jesus as the one who saves your people.

Leader: The angel said to Mary, "'[Your son] will be great, and will be called the Son of the Most High'" (1:32).

Group: Awesome God, Jesus truly is great. We believe that in him we will know you most clearly and intimately.

Leader: The angel of the Lord said to the shepherds, "'To you is born this day in the city of David a Savior, who is the Messiah, the Lord'" (2:11).

Group: Saving God, we are humbled that you would think so highly of us as to send your Son to be the one who would save us from sin and darkness.

Leader: To a righteous man, Simeon, it had been revealed by the Holy Spirit "that he would not see death before he had seen the Lord's Messiah" (2:26).

Group: Gracious God, may it be true of us that we will not see death until we have seen your Messiah, Christ, who redeems us now and for eternity.

Leader: Simeon said to the Lord, "'My eyes have seen your salvation, which you have prepared in the presence of all peoples, a light for revelation to the Gentiles and for glory to your people Israel'" (2:30–32).

Group: Welcoming God, how marvelous that you include all humanity within the bounds of your love and grace.

Leader: The prophet, Anna, upon seeing the child, Jesus, "began to praise God and to speak about the child to all who were looking for the redemption of Jerusalem" (2:38).

Group: Holy God, we with Anna praise you for Jesus. Help us to speak of him as the one who brings peace, justice, and hope to our world. Amen.

Comparing the Birth Narratives of John and Jesus

The Birth of John Luke 1:5–25, 57–80	Questions to Answer	The Birth of Jesus Luke 1:26–38; 2:1–20
1.	What are the circumstances of the foretelling of the birth? Who are the persons involved?	1.
2.	What is the response to the message brought by the angel regarding the birth?	2.
3.	How would you describe the mother-to-be?	3.
4.	What are the circumstances of the birth itself? Who are the characters involved?	4.
5.	What do you think the writer of Luke would want for us to understand regarding this particular birth?	5.

Session Two

Jesus Begins His Work

A Study of Luke 3:1–4:44

BEFORE THE SESSION

Focus of the Session

The focus for this session will be on the historical/political setting of Jesus' ministry and his baptism, genealogy, temptation, and preaching in Nazareth.

Advance Preparation

- Read the notes in a study Bible or commentary for Luke 3:1–4:44.

- Read chapter 2 in the Participant's Guide (pp. 18–24).

- Read articles in a Bible dictionary that deal with "John the Baptist," "Jesus' interpretation of the Law," "baptism," "temptation," and "synagogue."

- Try to obtain a large map of the land of Palestine during the time of Jesus' ministry to use in locating the various areas mentioned in the Participant's Guide.

- If you choose to sing the hymn at the end of the session, you will need to secure some hymnals or arrange to have the words of the hymn duplicated.

- Provide a few extra Bibles for those who forget to bring one.

DURING THE SESSION
Welcoming the Participants

Arrive at class early enough to set up the refreshments and have everything ready before the first persons arrive. If you used name tags in the first session, you will want to have them available again. Hopefully a few persons will show up who did not attend the first session. Be sure to welcome them warmly and assure them they will catch on quickly with the study of Luke and will be able to participate easily. If they did not bring a Bible, be sure to give them one to use during the class and give them a copy of this course book.

Opening Prayer

After words of welcome and introductions of any who are present for the first time, invite the participants to join you in prayer using the words of Psalm 119:1–16 as the basis for a litany. Introduce the time of prayer by stating that in an activity later in the session you will consider the event of Jesus' teaching in the synagogue in Nazareth, his hometown. Psalm 119 is an acrostic psalm in which every verse includes a synonym or metaphor for the word "law." Jesus' teaching surprised the people who knew him well. No doubt he taught from God's word in the Law and the Prophets, and that word from God could be unsettling. Invite the participants to turn to page 89 in the Leader's Guide. Divide the group in half, with one side reading the verses in plain text and the other side reading the alternating verses in italics.

Setting the Historical and Political Stage

Luke 3:1–2 is the writer's way of identifying the time of John the Baptist and Jesus. Take a few minutes to review the geography and political situation at the time of the beginnings of their ministries. Call attention to the following:

- Luke makes a quick transition between the boy Jesus in the temple (2:41–52) and introducing John, son of Zechariah (3:2).

- After Herod the Great died in 4 BCE, the jurisdiction of the land on the eastern coast of the Mediterranean was divided among his sons.

- If possible, arrange for a large map that shows the following territories: Judea, Galilee, Ituraea, Abilene, Samaria, and Judea.

- The sons ruled over the following territories: Herod Antipas, Galilee; Philip, the region of Ituraea, to the north of Galilee; Lysanias, ruler of Abilene, to the east of Ituraea; and Archelaus, ruler of Samaria, Judea, and Idumea, to the south of Galilee.

- The author of the Participant's Guide points out that Archelaus is not mentioned in the text, probably because his rule was a failure, so that by the time of John and Jesus, Rome had imposed a governor in his place. This governor was Pilate.

- In addition to the historical/political setting, Luke places the time in a religious setting, during the time of the high priests Annas and Caiaphas.

Comparing the John the Baptist Narratives

John the Baptist is presented in all four Gospels as the precursor to Jesus. Spend a few minutes guiding the group in an exploration of the differences as well as the similarities among the four Gospels.

- Divide the class into three sections. Assign one section Matthew 3:1–12; a second section, Mark 1:1–8; and the third section, John 1:15–28. In each section ask the members to work in pairs or threes.

- Direct the participants to page 90, the worksheet "Comparing the Narratives of John the Baptist."

- In pairs or threes focused on the assigned passage, have participants answer the seven questions.

- When they have finished answering the questions, return as a whole group to compare answers.

- Ask participants to turn to Luke 3:3–20 and keep a bookmark or finger at that place so that they will have the Luke narrative in front of them to compare with the other three.

- Answer one question at a time from the other three Gospels, and then look at Luke to see similarities and/or differences.

Conclude by discussing one or two questions:

- What do you see to be the importance of John's ministry?

- Why do you think Luke has included the information he has or excluded other points?

- What do you notice as unique to Luke's narrative?

Reviewing Jesus' Baptism, Genealogy, and Temptation

Summarize the baptism passage with comments such as the following:

- In Luke's Gospel the baptism of Jesus narrative is only two verses. We read that after Jesus had been baptized, he was praying, during which time the "heaven was opened, and the Holy Spirit descended upon him in bodily form like a dove" (3:21b–22).

- Matthew, in contrast to Luke and Mark, has John expressing some resistance to baptizing Jesus.

- Also in Matthew, the Spirit of God appears like a dove as he is coming up from the water, which is similar to the account in Mark.

- In Luke and Mark the voice from heaven says, " 'You are my Son, the Beloved; with you I am well pleased' " (Luke 3:22; Mark 1:11), whereas in Matthew the voice says, " 'This is my Son, the Beloved, with whom I am well pleased' " (Matt. 3:17). In John there is no voice from heaven, but John testifies that Jesus is the Son of God.

In the Gospels of Luke and Matthew there are two different genealogies of Jesus. Direct the class members to turn to Matthew 1:1–17, keep a bookmark at that place, and then turn to Luke 3:23–38. After they have had a few minutes to skim and compare the two genealogies, ask them to share what they notice as differences. If they have not identified the following, you can share what they have missed.

- Jesus' genealogy begins the Gospel of Matthew whereas in Luke it appears between his baptism and temptation.

- Luke states that "Jesus was about thirty years old when he began his work" (3:23a).

- Matthew begins, "An account of the genealogy of Jesus the Messiah, the son of David, the son of Abraham" (1:1), whereas Luke makes no mention of Jesus as Messiah.

- Matthew begins by tracing ancestors from Abraham to Jesus whereas Luke begins by tracing backwards from Jesus to Adam.

- In Matthew's genealogy, five women are mentioned (Tamar, Rehab, Ruth, Uriah, and Mary) whereas in Luke only men are mentioned.

As you did with the genealogy passages, direct the participants to turn to Matthew's account of Jesus' temptation (Matt. 4:1–11) and to Luke's account (4:1–13). Guide the group to see the similarities and differences. They should notice the following:

- Jesus was "led by the Spirit" into the wilderness.

- Jesus is tempted three times by the devil.

- The temptations are the same as are Jesus' answers to the devil.

- The second and third temptations are the same, but in reverse order.

- After Jesus was tempted, we read in Luke that the devil departed "until an opportune time." Matthew has a different conclusion: "Suddenly angels came and waited on him."

- Unless some of the participants have a Bible with cross-reference notes or a study Bible, the source of Jesus' answers will not be obvious when he says, " 'It is written. . . .' " Jesus is quoting from Deuteronomy, which is presented as Moses' "farewell message" to the Israelites just prior to his death and their crossing over the Jordan into the promised land.

- Jesus' answer to the temptation to turn stones into bread is quoted from Deuteronomy 8:3.

- His answer to the temptation to rule all the kingdoms of earth is from Deuteronomy 6:13.

- And his answer to the temptation to throw himself off the pinnacle of the temple is from Deuteronomy 6:16.

A key point to make is that the wilderness where Jesus is tempted is in the vicinity of the wilderness where the Israelites were encamped prior to their entry into the promised land. Just as the Israelites have endured a wilderness experience (forty years) before entering into a whole new era of service to God, so also Jesus has endured a wilderness experience (forty days) prior to launching into his faithful ministry of serving God and serving the people of God.

Exploring Jesus in the Synagogue in Nazareth

Guide the class members in an exploration of the narrative of Jesus preaching in the synagogue in Nazareth by doing the following:

- First call attention to several significant differences between Luke and the other three Gospels. In John there is no narrative of Jesus preaching in the synagogue in Nazareth. In Matthew's and Mark's Gospels the event is similar, quite short, and appears later in Jesus' ministry. The conclusion in Matthew and Mark is that Jesus was too well known by his friends and neighbors in Nazareth. They questioned his authority, and Jesus was unable to "do many deeds of power there, because of their unbelief" (Matt. 13:58; Mark 6:5).

- Luke's narrative is more extensive and is the first public act of Jesus' ministry. Jesus read the Scriptures from the prophet Isaiah and declared that he is the fulfillment of what the prophet proclaimed. At first, the people of Nazareth are quite taken by Jesus: "All spoke well of him and were amazed at the gracious words that came from his mouth" (4:22).

- Luke is similar to Matthew and Mark in that Jesus said, " 'Truly I tell you, no prophet is accepted in the prophet's hometown' " (4:24).

- Jesus got into trouble after he spoke about two narratives in the Hebrew Scriptures when he mentioned Elijah and the widow of Zarephath and Elisha and the cleansing of Naaman the Syrian of his leprosy.

- Divide the class in half. Assign one half the passage of Elijah and the widow of Zarephath (1 Kgs. 17:1–16) and the other half the passage of the cleansing of Naaman the Syrian (2 Kgs. 5:1–19).

- The members of each group are to read their assigned passage. It will help considerably if persons have study Bibles with notes regarding the circumstances of the widow of Zarephath and Naaman the general. If they do not have study Bibles, explain to each group that its key character was a non-Israelite, a nonbeliever in the God of Abraham, Isaac, and Jacob.

- The task of each group is to try to discern why Jesus' reference to their assigned passage was so disturbing to the members of the Nazareth synagogue that they decided they needed to get rid of Jesus.

After the two groups have read and discussed their assigned passages, lead a discussion guided by the following questions or questions you have created:

- What do you think God is trying to communicate to and through the prophet?

- How is the prophet serving God in the passage?

- What for you is the central teaching of the passage?

- Why do you suppose the people of Nazareth were so upset when Jesus reminded them of these two narratives?

- In what ways is this passage in Luke's Gospel relevant for us today?

Conclude this part of the session by looking quickly at the next acts of Jesus at the beginning of his ministry. Before calling his disciples, Jesus is in Capernaum where he teaches on the Sabbath, heals a man with an unclean spirit, heals Simon Peter's mother-in-law, and heals others with various diseases. Notice that Jesus "departed to a deserted place" (a recurring theme in Luke).

He continued proclaiming the "good news of the kingdom of God" in the synagogues of Judea.

Closing

If some in your group are familiar with the hymn "Love Divine, All Loves Excelling" and a person or two can lead in singing, conclude the session by singing the first stanza of the hymn. You could sing additional stanzas if you have hymnals available or have printed the words on a handout. If you choose not to sing, then read the words of the first stanza as a closing prayer.

> Love divine, all loves excelling, Joy of heaven to earth come down,
> Fix in us Thy humble dwelling, All Thy faithful mercies crown!
> Jesus, Thou art all compassion, Pure unbounded love Thou art;
> Visit us with Thy salvation, Enter every trembling heart.[1]

AFTER THE SESSION

Encourage the participants to read chapter 3 in the Participant's Guide and Luke 5:1–9:50 in preparation for the next class session.

Note

1. Charles Wesley, "Love Divine, All Loves Excelling," *Presbyterian Hymnal* (Louisville, KY: Westminster/John Knox Press, 1990), 376.

A Prayer

(Based on Psalm 119:1–16)

Happy are those whose way is blameless, who walk in the law of the Lord.

Happy are those who keep his decrees, who seek him with their whole heart,

who also do no wrong, but walk in his ways.

You have commanded your precepts to be kept diligently.

O that my ways may be steadfast in keeping your statutes!

Then I shall not be put to shame, having my eyes fixed on all your commandments.

I will praise you with an upright heart, when I learn your righteous ordinances.

I will observe your statutes; do not utterly forsake me.

How can young people keep their way pure? By guarding it according to your word.

With my whole heart I seek you; do not let me stray from your commandments.

I treasure your word in my heart, so that I may not sin against you.

Blessed are you, O Lord; teach me your statutes.

With my lips I declare all the ordinances of your mouth.

I delight in the way of your decrees as much as in all riches.

I will meditate on your precepts, and fix my eyes on your ways.

I will delight in your statutes; I will not forget your word.

Comparing the Narratives of John the Baptist			
	Matthew 3:1–12	**Mark 1:1–8**	**John 1:15–28**
1. What precedes the narrative that introduces John?			
2. What is the quote from Isaiah, if there is one?			
3. How is John's clothing described?			
4. Who comes to be baptized by John?			
5. What questions were raised about John? By whom?			
6. What did John say about the nature of his ministry?			
7. What happened to John?			

Jesus the Healer and Jesus at Work in Galilee

A Study of Luke 5:1–9:50

BEFORE THE SESSION
Focus of the Session

The focus for this session will be on many healing acts of Jesus and other miracles. In addition, part of the session deals with Jesus' disciples and the matter of discipleship.

Advance Preparation

- Read the notes in a study Bible or commentary for Luke 5:1–9:50.

- Read chapter 3 in the Participant's Guide (pp. 25–33).

- Read articles in a Bible dictionary that deal with "miracles of healing," "disciple," and "discipleship."

- Prepare comments on the several passages related to Jesus and his disciples.

- Choose a hymn for the closing of the session. If you decide to sing more than one stanza of a familiar hymn, you may need to arrange for hymnals or printed words of the hymn.

- Provide a few extra Bibles for those who forget to bring one.

DURING THE SESSION
Welcoming the Participants

Arrive at class early enough to set up the refreshments and have everything ready before the first persons arrive. If you used name tags in the first two sessions, you will want to have them available again. Hopefully a new person or two will show up who did not attend the previous sessions. Be sure to welcome them warmly and assure them they will catch on quickly with the study of Luke and will be able to participate easily. If they did not bring a Bible, be sure to give them one to use during the class and give them a copy of this course book.

Opening Prayer

After words of welcome and introductions of any who are present for the first time, invite the participants to join in the opening prayer. We are focusing on a psalm again, primarily because Psalms was Jesus' prayer book and the psalms are as relevant for our spiritual life today as they were for Jesus in his day. Lead the group through the following steps:

- Direct the participants to page 96 in the Leader's Guide for the opening prayer in the words of Psalm 40:1–8.

- Ask them to read silently the prayer from Psalm 40 and to select one or two lines or verses that speak to them in a special way.

- After time for reading, check to see if everyone has selected a line or verse or two.

- Invite participants to take turns sharing the words of Psalm 40:1–8 that are most meaningful to them.

- In response to each person's sharing, ask everyone to say in unison, "Hear our prayer, O Lord."

Reviewing Six Short Stories

In Luke 5:1–6:11 we encounter six short stories. Guide the class in reviewing these six stories by using the following process:

- Ask the members of the class to work in pairs.

- Direct them to page 97 of the Leader's Guide, "Reviewing Six Short Stories."

- Each pair is to select one story with which to work so that the pairs are working with different stories. If you have fewer than twelve participants, you could skip a story or two, or several people could work individually. If you have more than twelve, they could work in small groups of three or more.

- The directions are on the worksheet: to read the assigned passage and to discuss the three questions.

- After the pairs or small groups have finished their work, ask the participants to form groups of six persons, each person with a different one of the six stories.

- Their task in the new group of six is to retell the story in sequence. Ask them to speak using first-person point of view and retell the story from the perspective of one of the characters mentioned in the story.

- When the groups of six have completed retelling the short stories, lead them in a discussion guided by a question such as "What do you think Luke was attempting to communicate to the readers of his Gospel about the person Jesus?"

Considering Jesus and His Disciples

A number of passages in this section of Luke feature Jesus with his disciples. Perhaps the best way to proceed with this topic is to provide a quick overview of the significant passages by leading the participants through a time of reading and commenting on the following:

- Jesus calls three fishermen to follow him (5:1–11).

- Jesus calls a tax collector to follow him (5:27–32).

- Jesus chooses twelve apostles (6:12–16).

- Jesus calms a storm when the disciples are frightened (8:22–25).

- Jesus sends the Twelve on a mission (9:1–6).

- Jesus asks the disciples about his identity (9:18–20).

- Jesus is transfigured in the presence of three disciples (9:28–36).

- Jesus speaks about true greatness (9:46–48).

- Jesus speaks about true followers (9:57–62).

After reading these passages and offering a few comments, engage the participants in a discussion prompted by several questions such as the following or others you have created:

- What do you observe in these passages regarding the relationship between Jesus and his disciples?

- What do think is the main point Luke wants to communicate about Jesus and his disciples?

- What is the relevance of these passages for understanding the nature of discipleship today?

Exploring Jesus' Ministry of Healing

In Luke chapters 7 to 9 there are seven narratives in which Jesus heals and/or forgives those who seek him out. The plan is again to work in pairs or small groups, each focused on just one of the narratives. After you have made an introduction to Jesus' healing ministry, guide the class members through the following process:

- Form small groups of two to four persons.

- Direct the participants to page 98 in the Leader's Guide, "Jesus' Ministry of Healing."

- Each small group is to select one of the passages and to answer the questions found on the worksheet.

- After they have read the passages and answered the questions, work with the participants in the large group to share their answers to the last question on the worksheet: "What insights come to you from this passage regarding Jesus?"

- Conclude the discussion by asking another question: "In what ways can we interpret these healing narratives and apply their meaning to faith and life today?"

Closing

One of the key concepts of this session is "discipleship." Conclude your session by singing the first stanza of a familiar hymn that speaks of our discipleship. Possible hymns to choose from include "Lord, I Want to Be a Christian," "What a Friend We Have in Jesus," "Take My Life and Let It Be," "O Master, Let Me Walk with Thee," and "Take Thou Our Minds, Dear Lord." If you have access to hymnals, you may want to sing more than one stanza.

AFTER THE SESSION

Encourage the participants to read chapter 4 in the Participant's Guide and Luke 9:51–19:27 in preparation for the next class session.

A Prayer

(Psalm 40:1–8)

I waited patiently for the LORD;
    he inclined to me and heard my cry.
He drew me up from the desolate pit,
    out of the miry bog,
and set my feet upon a rock,
    making my steps secure.
He put a new song in my mouth,
    a song of praise to our God.
Many will see and fear,
    and put their trust in the LORD.

Happy are those who make
    the LORD their trust,
who do not turn to the proud,
    to those who go astray after false gods.
You have multiplied, O LORD my God,
    your wondrous deeds and your thoughts toward us;
    none can compare with you.
Were I to proclaim and tell of them,
    they would be more than can be counted.

Sacrifice and offering you do not desire,
    but you have given me an open ear.
Burnt offering and sin offering
    you have not required.
Then I said, "Here I am;
    in the scroll of the book it is written of me.
I delight to do your will, O my God;
    your law is within my heart."

Reviewing Six Short Stories

Directions: Work in pairs, with each pair selecting one of the following stories from Luke. After reading the short story, discuss the several questions below. Be prepared to retell your story in your own words.

Six Short Stories:

A Nature Miracle (5:1–11)
A Healing Miracle with an Orthodox Conclusion (5:12–16)
A Healing Miracle with an Unorthodox Conclusion (5:17–26)
Jesus Dines in Questionable Company (5:27–39)
Jesus Again Pushes the Boundaries (6:1–5)
Jesus Teaches and Heals on the Sabbath (6:6–11)

Questions to Discuss:

1. Who are the main characters in the story?

_____

_____

2. What did Jesus' action communicate about his ministry?

_____

_____

3. What do we, and those in the story, learn about Jesus?

_____

_____

Jesus' Ministry of Healing

Directions: Work in pairs, with each pair selecting one of the following stories from Luke. After reading the short story, answer the several questions below.

Seven Healing Narratives:
  Jesus Heals a Centurion's Servant (7:1–10)
  Jesus Raises a Widow's Son (7:11–17)
  Jesus Forgives a Sinful Woman (7:36–50)
  Jesus Heals the Gerasene Demoniac (8:26–39)
  Jesus Restores to Life a Young Girl (8:40–42a, 49–56)
  Jesus Heals a Woman with a Hemorrhage (8:42b–48)
  Jesus Heals a Boy with a Demon (9:37–43a)

Questions to Discuss:

1. What is the circumstance of the person in need?

_____

_____

2. How does Jesus respond to the one in need and/or to others?

_____

_____

3. What is the response of the one Jesus heals or forgives?

_____

_____

4. What is the response of others who are present?

_____

_____

5. What insights come to you from this passage regarding Jesus?

_____

_____

Session Four

Jesus the Teacher and His Journey to Jerusalem

A Study of Luke 9:51–19:27

BEFORE THE SESSION

Focus of the Session

The central focus of this session is on Jesus as teacher and the primary method he used for teaching—parables. The class will be led to explore ten different parables and then focus as a whole class on one parable. Depending on how much time you have, you may be able to highlight some of the other significant narratives in this section of Luke.

Advance Preparation

- Read the notes in a study Bible or commentary for Luke 9:51–19:27.

- Read chapter 4 in the Participant's Guide, 34–42.

- Read articles in a Bible dictionary that deal with "parable," "Samaritan," and "Zacchaeus."

- Prepare comments that you would like to share related to the several narratives in the activity before the closing.

- If you choose to ask questions other than the ones suggested by the author, take time to prepare them ahead of time. Analytical and personalized questions will prompt the most discussion.

- If you choose to deal with the "journey" aspect of these ten chapters, it will be helpful if you are able to obtain a map of Palestine at the time of Jesus.

- Provide a few extra Bibles for those who forget to bring one.

DURING THE SESSION
Welcoming the Participants

After three sessions your class should be pretty well settled and familiar with the routine of getting their name tags and signing in (if that is your practice). Be sure that refreshments are prepared ahead of time and that you have a couple of extra Bibles and copies of this course book available for those who did not bring theirs. Greet participants by name as they arrive and engage them in general conversation about what they have been reading and thinking regarding their study of Luke's Gospel.

Opening Prayer

When it is time to begin, call everyone together to open the session with prayer. The Lord's Prayer is one of the topics of this week's study. Guide the group through the following few steps as they interact with Luke's version of the prayer.

- Direct the participants to the worksheet on page 105 in the Leader's Guide for "Responding to Luke's Version of the Lord's Prayer."

- Review the instructions and emphasize that there are no "correct" or "incorrect" words to be written, just words that are personal thoughts of the participants.

- After time for writing, take a few minutes for participants who are willing to share what they have written.

- Begin the sharing by first reading the line from Luke and then pause to allow for those who have written something to share what they created.

- After one or more have shared, move on to the next line from Luke.

- Conclude by praying together in unison Luke's version of the Lord's Prayer.

Considering Parables

A major feature of these ten chapters of Luke's Gospel is the presentation by Jesus of many parables. Before exploring several of the parables, it will be important to consider the nature of parables. Make a brief presentation to include the following points:

- First, ask class members what they think of when they hear the word *parable*.

- Accept all the responses, and then share a dictionary definition of *parable*.

- Distinguish parables from similes and metaphors, and mention that Jesus used all three types of speech in his teaching.

- Emphasize that parables were a primary teaching method used by Jesus.

- Remind the participants that parables have multiple layers of meaning and that there is no one, correct interpretation of a parable. This will set the stage for what follows as they are invited to explore a parable to discern what it means.

Exploring Ten Parables

A number of passages in this section of Luke can be identified as parables. We cannot deal with all of the parables in this activity, but we can explore six to ten of them. Guide the participants in this activity with the following directions:

- Direct the participants to the worksheet on page 106 in the Leader's Guide, "Exploring Ten Parables."

- Ask them to work in pairs or threes; each small group is to work on just one parable.

- They are to read the parable and then answer the four questions on the worksheet.

- After the small groups have finished their work, organize the class into different small groups of three or four persons. There should be three or four different parables represented by the persons in the group.

- The task of the newly formed small groups is to compare notes by first summarizing their parables and then answering one question at a time.

Conclude this activity by discussing with the whole group one or more of the following questions or others you have prepared:

- What have you learned about Jesus as a teacher by exploring these parables?

- In many ways Jesus' teachings were quite radical; what is so radical about these teachings of Jesus in the parables?

- What is the relevance of Jesus' teaching in these parables for us today?

Reflecting on the Parable of the Loving Father

One of the most familiar of Jesus' parables is the one commonly referred to as the parable of the Prodigal Son. I think it is even more appropriate to identify this as the parable of the Loving Father because there are two sons in the parable and the father's love is offered equally to each. The main point of the parable is what the father does, not what the younger son does. Engage the participants in the following process:

- Direct the participants to page 107 in the Leader's Guide, "The Parable of the Loving Father."

- Introduce this parable with a few comments you have prepared, based on your notes from commentary or study Bible.

- Ask for volunteers to read the parts of narrator, father, and servant. For the roles of the two sons, assign half of the remainder of the class to be the younger son and the other half to be the elder son.

- Conduct the dramatic reading.

After the reading, spend a few minutes discussing two or more of the following questions or ones that you have created:

- What did you hear or see in this reading of the parable that seemed to be new or a different perspective on the familiar parable?

- What did it feel like to be the younger son or the elder son?

- What are some ways that you see this as a radical teaching of Jesus?

- The author of the Leader's Guide labeled this the "parable of the Loving Father." What do you think of that as a title compared to the traditional identification as the parable of the Prodigal Son?

- What do you think is the main point Jesus is trying to make with this parable?

- If you had been one of the Pharisees in the audience, what would you have thought about what Jesus was saying?

- What are some implications for applying Jesus' teaching in this parable to life and faith today?

Reviewing Other Parts of Luke's Narrative

In these ten chapters of Luke there are several important narratives that are not parables. Take a few minutes to skim through several of the following narratives by making a few pertinent comments about those you choose to emphasize.

- Jesus appoints, instructs, and sends the seventy followers (10:1–24).

- Jesus visits Mary and Martha (10:38–42).

- Jesus heals a crippled woman (13:10–17).

- Jesus laments over Jerusalem (13:31–35).

- Jesus cleanses ten lepers (17:11–19).

- The rich ruler asks Jesus a question (18:18–30).

- Jesus heals a blind beggar (18:35–43).

- Jesus goes to the house of Zacchaeus (19:1–10).

Closing

We began the session with Luke's version of the Lord's Prayer. For our closing we will pray another version of the Lord's Prayer, known as the ecumenical version. Direct the class members to page 108 of the Leader's Guide, "The Lord's Prayer: Ecumenical Version." Before praying the prayer in unison, ask the participants to read the words and compare them with Luke's version and with the traditional version that they usually pray. What do they notice about the differences among the three prayers? Conclude by praying in unison the ecumenical version.

AFTER THE SESSION

Encourage the participants to read chapter 5 in the Participant's Guide and Luke 19:28–22:38 in preparation for the next class session.

Responding to Luke's Version of the Lord's Prayer

Directions: Printed below are the words of Luke's version of the Lord's Prayer (Luke 11:2–4). Your task is to write some words in the boxes that are prompted by the words of the prayer. Write what comes to mind either in the way of a paraphrase or just your own response to what the words of Jesus mean to you. Try to fill in two or three of the boxes with your words.

"Father, hallowed be your name."

"Your kingdom come."

"Give us each day our daily bread."

"And forgive us our sins,"

"for we ourselves forgive everyone indebted to us."

"And do not bring us to the time of trial."

Exploring Ten Parables

Directions: Working in pairs, each pair will select one of the following parables from Luke. After reading the parable answer the several questions below.

Ten Parables of Jesus:
Good Samaritan (10:30–37)
Friend at Midnight (11:5–8)
Wise and Faithful Servants (12:42–48)
Barren Fig Tree (13:6–9)
Mustard Seed and Yeast (13:18–21)
The Great Dinner (14:16–24)
The Lost Sheep (15:1–7)
The Lost Coin (15:8–10)
The Widow and the Unjust Judge (18:1–8)
Pharisee and Tax Collector (18:9–14)

Questions to Discuss:

1. Looking at what comes before and after the parable, what is the context of Jesus' teaching?

_____

_____

2. To whom does it appear Jesus is addressing the parable?

_____

_____

3. What do you discern as the main point of the parable?

_____

_____

4. What is the relevance of the parable for believers today?

_____

_____

The Parable of the Loving Father

(Adapted from Luke 15:11–32)

Narrator:	Jesus also told them another story: Once a man had two sons. The younger son said to his father,
Young Son:	"Give me my share of the property."
Narrator:	So the father divided his property between his two sons. Not long after that, the younger son packed up everything he owned and left for a foreign country, where he wasted all his money in wild living. He had spent everything when a bad famine spread through that whole land. Soon he had nothing to eat. He went to work for a man in that country, and the man sent him out to take care of his pigs. He would have been glad to eat what the pigs were eating, but no one gave him a thing. Finally, he came to his senses and said,
Young Son:	"My father's workers have plenty to eat, and here I am, starving to death! I will go to my father and say to him, 'Father, I have sinned against God in heaven and against you. I am no longer good enough to be called your son. Treat me like one of your workers.'"
Narrator:	The younger son got up and started back to his father. But when he was still a long way off, his father saw him and felt sorry for him. He ran to his son and hugged and kissed him.
Young Son:	"Father, I have sinned against God in heaven and against you. I am no longer good enough to be called your son."
Narrator:	But his father said to the servants,
Father:	"Hurry and bring the best clothes and put them on him. Give him a ring for his finger and sandals for his feet. Get the best calf and prepare it, so we can eat and celebrate. This son of mine was dead, but has now come back to life. He was lost and has now been found."
Narrator:	And they began to celebrate. The older son had been out in the field. But when he came near the house, he heard the music and dancing. So he called one of the servants over and asked,
Older Son:	"What's going on here?"
Servant:	"Your brother has come home safe and sound, and your father ordered us to kill the best calf."
Narrator:	The older brother got so angry that he would not even go into the house. His father came out and begged him to go in. But he said to his father,
Older Son:	"For years I have worked for you like a slave and have always obeyed you. But you have never even given me a little goat, so that I could give a dinner for my friends. This other son of yours wasted your money on prostitutes. And now that he has come home, you ordered the best calf to be killed for a feast."
Father:	"My son, you are always with me, and everything I have is yours. But we should be glad and celebrate! Your brother was dead, but he is now alive. He was lost and has now been found."

The Lord's Prayer: Ecumenical Version

Our Father in heaven,
hallowed be your name.
Your kingdom come,
your will be done on earth as in heaven.
Give us today our daily bread.
Forgive us our sins
as we forgive those who sin against us.
Save us from the time of trial
and deliver us from evil.
For the kingdom, the power, and the glory are yours
now and forever. Amen.

Session Five

Jesus in Jerusalem

A Study of Luke 19:28–22:38

BEFORE THE SESSION
Focus of the Session

There is a lot of material to cover in this session, which will include two activities that involve comparing passages from Luke with two or three of the Synoptic Gospels: those involving Jesus' entry into Jerusalem and the Last Supper. A major activity will be the exploration of six passages that represent hard teachings of Jesus.

Advance Preparation

- Read the notes in a study Bible or commentary for Luke 19:28–22:38.

- Read chapter 5 in the Participant's Guide (pp. 43–49).

- Read articles in a Bible dictionary that deal with "temple" and "Passover."

- It would be helpful for you to prepare answers to all the questions in the first activity comparing the Luke and Matthew narratives of Jesus' entry into Jerusalem so that you have identified all the differences and similarities ahead of time.

- Check the notes in a commentary or study Bible related to the six passages to be explored in the activity "Six Hard Teachings of Jesus."

- Provide a few extra Bibles for those who forget to bring one.

DURING THE SESSION
Opening Prayer

Invite the participants to join you in prayer, which is in the form of a litany. Introduce the prayer by stating that in the Luke chapters for this session there are several sayings of Jesus that will prompt our prayers. (The words of Jesus are presented below.) After each saying the group is to respond in unison, "O God, help me understand Jesus' words." You could write the response on a sheet of newsprint for all to see.

- Jesus quoted the prophet Isaiah, saying, " 'It is written, "My house shall be a house of prayer" ' " (19:46).

- Jesus said, " 'Give to the emperor the things that are the emperor's, and to God the things that are God's' " (20:25).

- Jesus said, " 'Truly I tell you, this poor widow has put in more than all of them; for all of them have contributed out of their abundance, but she out of her poverty has put in all she had to live on' " (21:3–4).

- Jesus said, " 'I have eagerly desired to eat this Passover with you before I suffer; for I tell you, I will not eat it until it is fulfilled in the kingdom of God' " (22:15–16).

- Jesus said, " 'This is my body, which is given for you. Do this in remembrance of me' " (22:19).

- Jesus said, " 'This cup that is poured out for you is the new covenant in my blood' " (22:20).

- Jesus said, "'The greatest among you must become like the youngest, and the leader like one who serves'" (22:26).

Comparing Luke's and Matthew's Narratives of Jesus' Entry into Jerusalem

The author of the Participant's Guide calls attention to some of the differences between Luke's and Matthew's narratives of Jesus' entry into Jerusalem. In this activity you will guide the participants to see and reflect on these differences. This process will be a good way to focus on the story line of the narratives.

Divide the class into two groups. One group will focus on Matthew 21:1–17, and the other group, on Luke 19:28–48. To guide the comparing of the narratives ask the questions that follow, and then invite persons in each group to give their answers.

- What locations are identified where the events took place?

- What animal or animals are mentioned?

- Is there a quote from a prophet? If so, what is the quote?

- What does Jesus ride on?

- What is laid on the animals and on the road?

- What do the people shout? (Refer to Psalm 118:26–27.)

- What is the state of the city of Jerusalem at this time?

- What is the response of the religious authorities? Which authorities are mentioned?

- What does Jesus do when he comes near the city of Jerusalem?

- What does Jesus do and say when he enters the temple in Jerusalem?

- What does Jesus do and say after overturning the tables of the money changers?

- Where does Jesus spend the night(s)?

In the process of answering the questions the participants will become aware of many differences between the two Gospels. After completing the comparison, guide the group in a discussion guided by several questions:

- What are some of your impressions after seeing all the differences between Matthew and Luke?

- This narrative is often referred to as a triumphal entry. In what sense is it triumphal? Or do you think that it is not so triumphal? Why or why not?

- What do you make of the responses of the various characters in the narratives: the crowd, religious leaders, and disciples?

- If you had been among the crowd on that day, what are some thoughts or feelings you might have had?

- On the next Palm Sunday, what might you be looking for in the liturgy or expecting to hear in the sermon?

Exploring Some Hard Teachings of Jesus

There are six passages in this section that reflect hard teachings of Jesus. Divide your class into six small groups. Direct the participants to page 114 of the Leader's Guide for the worksheet "Six Hard Teachings of Jesus." If you have fewer than twelve in your class, you can omit one or more of the passages. Lead them through the following steps:

- Each small group will work on one of the passages.

- After all have had time to read the passage and discuss the three questions, bring everyone back to the large group.

- Ask each small group to report its answers to the first two questions.

- Engage the whole group in discussing the third question.

Reflecting on the Last Supper

As you did with the entry-into-Jerusalem passage, spend some time comparing the three Synoptic Gospels regarding Jesus' last supper with his disciples. Lead the participants through the following steps:

- Divide the class into three groups.

- Assign each group one of the following passages: Luke 22:7–23; Matthew 26:17–30; and Mark 14:12–26.

- Ask someone from the group reading Luke to read the passage aloud while the members of the other two groups follow along with their passages.

- After the reading, go back to the beginning to "walk through" the passage with persons in the other two groups naming the differences and similarities that they see in their passages from Matthew and Mark.

Conclude this part of the session by discussing another question or two.

- What do you discern as the central truth the three Gospel writers are seeking to communicate?

- Jesus says, " 'This is my body, which is given for you' " and " 'This cup that is poured out for you is the new covenant in my blood.' " What do you think Jesus means by those two phrases?

- Which of these passages connects you most closely with your church's celebration of the Lord's Supper?

Closing

Conclude your session by singing or reading in unison the words of one or more stanzas of a hymn for Palm Sunday, "Ride On! Ride On in Majesty!

> Ride on! Ride on in majesty! Hark! all the tribes hosanna cry;
> O Savior meek, pursue Thy road With palms and scattered garments strowed.
>
> Ride on! Ride on in majesty! In lowly pomp ride on to die:
> O Christ, Thy triumphs now begin O'er captive death and conquered sin.
>
> Ride on! Ride on in majesty! The winged squadrons of the sky
> Look down with sad and wondering eyes To see the approaching sacrifice.
>
> Ride on! Ride on in majesty! In lowly pomp ride on to die;
> Bow Thy meek head to mortal pain, Then take, O God, Thy power, and reign.[1]

AFTER THE SESSION

Encourage the participants to read chapter 6 in the Participant's Guide and Luke 22:39–23:56 in preparation for the next class session.

Note

1. Henry Hart Milman, "Ride On! Ride On in Majesty!" *Presbyterian Hymnal* (Louisville, KY: Westminster/John Knox Press, 1990), 90 and 91.

Six Hard Teachings of Jesus

Directions: Working in pairs, each pair will select one of the following passages. After reading the passage answer the several questions below.

Six Hard Teachings of Jesus:
    Parable of the Wicked Tenants (20:9–19)
    A Question about Paying Taxes (20:20–26)
    A Question about the Resurrection (20:27–40)
    Signs of Things to Come (21:5–24)
    A Lesson from a Fig Tree (21:25–35)
    A Dispute about Greatness (22:24–30)

Questions to Discuss:

1. What are the meanings/implications of the images or metaphors Jesus used in the passage?

_____

_____

2. What do you think Jesus is trying to communicate?

_____

_____

3. How do you interpret this passage for our faith and life today?

_____

_____

Session Six

The Arrest, Trial, and Death of Jesus

A Study of Luke 22:39–23:56

BEFORE THE SESSION
Focus of the Session

In this session we will be dealing with the many episodes of the arrest, trial, and death of Jesus. The first activity will help provide background for understanding the dynamics at work in Jesus' arrest and trial. Even though there are only two narratives directly related to Peter, we will spend time focusing on the character of Peter and his relationship with Jesus as reflected in other passages in Luke. We will also retell the larger narrative of Jesus' arrest, trial, and crucifixion through twelve episodes in the narrative.

Advance Preparation

- Read the notes in a study Bible or commentary for Luke 22:39–23:56.

- Read chapter 6 in the Participant's Guide (pp. 50–57).

- Read articles in a Bible dictionary that deal with "Mount of Olives," "Pilate," "Herod," and "crucifixion."

- Look at the context of all the passages listed in the Setting the Stage activity and be prepared to make brief comments about the context of each.

- Provide a few extra Bibles for those who forget to bring one.

DURING THE SESSION
Opening Prayer

The author of the Participant's Guide writes (p. 51) about the importance of the word "remember" toward the end of Luke's Gospel. For the opening prayer, invite persons to try to remember where they were at the time of a major event in the community or the nation. Begin by asking, "Where were you, and what were you doing when . . . ?" After a brief time of sharing, make a few comments about the importance of memory and remembering. Then offer a prayer of thanksgiving for our memory and remembering:

> *Great and Gracious God, we come to you this day with thanksgiving for your presence with us in the life, death, and resurrection of Jesus the Christ, our savior. Thank you for the gift of memory that enables us to remember significant moments in our lives. Especially, we thank you for all those who remember your word for us in Holy Scripture that gives direction and meaning for our lives. Amen.*

Setting the Stage for Jesus' Trial

Before we look at the trial of Jesus and his crucifixion, it will be helpful to set the stage for that study by reviewing passages that help us understand why Jesus was a threat to the religious leaders. From the early chapters of Luke there are times when Jesus alluded to his time of trial and suffering as well as occasions when his opponents sought to be rid of him. In this activity you will review with class members the thirteen passages that follow. Lead the class from one passage to another, calling attention to the examples of hostility toward Jesus and to Jesus' own words reflecting on what he expects to happen. Be sure to comment briefly regarding the context of each passage.

- After preaching in Nazareth, Jesus is driven out of town (4:28–30).

- The Pharisees question Jesus (5:21).

- Jesus makes first statement about his death and resurrection (9:21–27).

- Jesus makes second statement about his trials (9:43b–45).

- Scribes and Pharisees are hostile toward Jesus (11:53–54).

- Jesus puts his opponents to shame (13:15–17).

- Pharisees watch Jesus closely (14:1–6).

- Pharisees and scribes grumble about Jesus' actions (15:1–2).

- Pharisees ridicule Jesus (16:14).

- Jesus makes third statement about his death and resurrection (18:31–34).

- Religious leaders look for a way to kill Jesus (19:45–48).

- Religious leaders want to lay hands on Jesus (20:19)

- Religious leaders plot to kill Jesus (22:1–2).

After you have worked your way through the thirteen passages, guide the class in a brief discussion prompted by questions such as the following or those you have created:

- We have looked at specific passages reflecting the hostility of the religious leaders. What are some examples of Jesus' teachings or actions that would cause the religious leaders to want to do away with Jesus?

- If you had been present as one of Jesus' disciples, what are some thoughts you might have had? What might you have said to Jesus when he spoke about his pending death and resurrection?

- What do you think Luke is seeking to communicate to the readers and hearers of his words about Jesus?

- How do you relate these words of Jesus and the responses to him by the religious leaders to our faith and life today?

Reflecting on the Apostle Peter

In Luke as in the other Gospels the apostle Peter plays a major role. He is often seen as the spokesman for the others. In this section of Luke we read of Jesus predicting that Peter would deny him, and then we read the narrative of his denial. In addition to this account we are going to focus on other passages in Luke involving Peter in order to get a sense of his character and his role as a follower of Jesus.

- Direct the participants to the worksheet on page 120 in the Leader's Guide, "Reflecting on the Apostle Peter."

- Organize the class into small groups of two or three persons. There are eight passages. If you have fewer than sixteen in the class, omit one or more of the passages.

- The small groups will read their assigned passage and answer the three questions.

- After they have finished their reading and discussing, return to the large group, where each small group will report its answers to the three questions.

- Ask the whole group to reflect together on a follow-up question: "What can we learn from Peter's relationship with Jesus to help us understand our relationship with him?"

Retelling the Trials and Crucifixion Narratives

There are a dozen important episodes in the narratives of Luke 22 and 23. In this activity each person will focus on one episode to read and then retell for the other class members. Be sure to allow enough time for the class members to complete the tasks outlined in the following steps:

- Direct the class members to the worksheet on page 121, "Twelve Episodes in the Trials and Crucifixion of Jesus."

- Assign each person one of the episodes and its related verses. (If you do not have twelve persons, either combine a couple of the events or eliminate as many as necessary. If you have more than twelve, it would be okay to assign two or more persons to an episode.)

- Ask each person to read his or her assigned verses and

to make note of the key persons, events, and words featured in the passage.

- After time for reading, ask the class members to retell the story in their own words. Encourage them not to read the passage from their Bibles but to use their imaginations to creatively retell their portion of the trials and crucifixion narrative.

When the individuals have completed their reading and reflection on the twelve episodes, guide the group in a discussion that could include questions such as the following:

- Look again at your assigned passage. What, for you, is a line or verse that stands out? Share the line or verse and state why it stands out for you.

- What aspect of your part of the narrative do you identify with personally?

- What aspects of the passage are troublesome for you? In what sense?

- What is the "bottom line" message that we can derive from the whole narrative of Luke 22 and 23?

Closing

For the closing sing one or more stanzas of "Were You There?"

> Were you there when they crucified my Lord?
> Were you there when they nailed him to the tree?
> Were you there when they pierced him in the side?
> Were you there when they laid him in the tomb?[1]

AFTER THE SESSION

Encourage the participants to read chapter 7 in the Participant's Guide and Luke 24:1–53 in preparation for the last class session.

Note

1. "Were You There?" *Presbyterian Hymnal* (Louisville, KY: Westminster/ John Knox Press, 1990), 102.

Reflecting on the Apostle Peter

Directions: Working in pairs, each pair will select one of the following stories from Luke. After reading the passage answer the several questions below.

Narratives where Peter is a key character:
>   Peter is called and included among the Twelve (5:1–11, 6:14).
>   Peter speaks up at healing of a woman and a girl (8:40–56).
>   Peter declares Jesus as Messiah (9:18–20).
>   Peter is present at the transfiguration of Jesus (9:28–36).
>   Peter is present when Jesus encounters a rich ruler (18:18–30).
>   The disciples prepare for and share the Passover meal with Jesus (22:7–23).
>   Jesus predicts Peter's denial (22:31–34).
>   Peter denies Jesus three times (22:54–62).

Questions to Discuss:

1. What is the context of Peter's encounter with Jesus?

_____

_____

2. What is Peter's role in the narrative?

_____

_____

3. What clues do you get from this passage regarding Peter's character?

_____

_____

Twelve Episodes in the Trials and Crucifixion of Jesus

Directions: Read your assigned passage and prepare to retell in your own words the important features of that part of the trials and crucifixion narrative. A little "divine imagination" is encouraged. This should take about ten minutes.

Jesus prays on the Mount of Olives (22:39–46).

Jesus is betrayed and arrested (22:47–53).

Peter denies Jesus (22:54–62).

Jesus is mocked and taken before the council (22:63–71).

Jesus stands before Pilate (23:1–5).

Jesus stands before Herod (23:6–12).

Jesus is sentenced to death (23:13–25).

Jesus is taken to the cross (23:26–31).

Jesus is crucified on the cross (23:32–38).

Two criminals are crucified with Jesus (23:39–43).

Jesus commends his spirit and breathes his last (23:44–49).

Joseph of Arimathea buries Jesus (23:50–56).

Session Seven

Resurrection and Ascension

A Study of Luke 24:1–53

BEFORE THE SESSION
Focus of the Session

This session focuses on just one chapter of Luke's Gospel, chapter 24, and deals with three major narratives: the women's visit to the empty tomb, the two disciples' walk on the road to Emmaus, and the resurrection appearance of Jesus in the midst of the disciples.

Advance Preparation

- Read the notes in a study Bible or commentary for Luke 24:1–53.

- Read chapter 7 in the Participant's Guide (pp. 58–65).

- Read articles in a Bible dictionary that deal with "meals with Jesus," "resurrection," and "ascension."

- For the Opening Prayer activity, review Luke's Gospel and make a list of all the meals Jesus shared with his disciples and others so that you can fill in the blanks of those that the participants have overlooked.

- In the Closing there is a suggestion to play the last movement of Beethoven's Ninth Symphony, the "Ode to Joy." If you plan to do this, you will need to arrange for a CD recording and to have a computer or player with speakers in order to present this piece as part of the closing.

- Also in the Closing there is a suggestion of using the words from the first line of the hymn "Joyful, Joyful, We Adore Thee" as a litany response. It would be helpful to print out the words on a sheet of newsprint for all to see.

- Depending on how much time you have, there may be one too many activities for this session, so you will have to decide which activity to omit or plan a way to do a couple of the activities differently and more quickly.

- Provide a few extra Bibles for those who forget to bring one.

DURING THE SESSION
Welcoming the Participants

One way to welcome the participants to this last session is to provide some special refreshments.

Opening Prayer

After everyone has gathered and while you are having refreshments, share a few comments about one of the features of Luke's Gospel—meals with Jesus. Invite the participants to suggest as many passages as they can remember where Jesus shared a meal with his disciples and/or others. There are two occasions of Jesus eating with others in Luke 24: in the evening on the walk to Emmaus and when he joined the disciples later in Jerusalem. After you and the group have mentioned a number of meals with Jesus, invite the participants to offer their own prayers of thanksgiving. Prompt the prayers by asking, "For what are you thankful as a result of your reading, discussing, and studying Luke's Gospel?" In response to each brief prayer of thanksgiving ask everyone to say in unison, "O God, we praise you with grateful hearts."

Comparing the Empty-Tomb Narratives in Four Gospels

The author of the Participant's Guide writes, "It was probably the case that the resurrection of Jesus had such a seminal and powerful influence on Jesus' disciples that it simply could not be fully described in just one story." It will be helpful to spend a few minutes comparing the four narratives. This activity is similar to one you have done before. Divide the class into four groups and assign a different passage to each group—Group 1: Matthew 28:1–10; Group 2: Mark 16:1–8; Group 3: Luke 24:1–12; and Group 4: John 20:1–10. To guide the comparing of the narratives, ask the questions that follow, and then invite persons in each group to give their answers.

- Who went to the tomb?
- When did they go?
- What did they find?
- Whom did they encounter?
- What was said to the one(s) who went to the tomb?
- How did they respond emotionally?
- What did they say and/or do?
- Who else went to the tomb?

After receiving responses to all of the questions from each of the groups, spend a few minutes guiding a discussion using questions such as those that follow or ones you have prepared.

- What do you notice to be unique to Luke's Gospel compared to the other three?
- Of the variety of responses by those who found the tomb empty, which response do you identify with most closely?
- What, if anything, perplexes you about these empty-tomb narratives?

Conclude this activity by sharing some of your understanding regarding the concept of resurrection based on notes you have made from your reading in a study Bible, commentary, and/or Bible dictionary.

"Walking" the Walk to Emmaus

The intent of this activity is to enable the participants to connect cognitively and emotionally with the two disciples of Jesus who are walking from Jerusalem to Emmaus. Guide the class members through Luke 24:13–35 by calling attention to the following points and asking several questions for a little discussion along the way:

- "That same day" is the first day of the week.

- "Two of them" refers to two followers of Jesus: one is Cleopas, but the other is not named. A traditional icon shows Jesus with a man and a woman, perhaps Cleopas's wife.

- Emmaus is seven miles from Jerusalem. It would be helpful if you could obtain a map of Palestine at the time of Jesus to show where Emmaus was.

- They were "talking with each other about all these things that had happened." What are some of the things they might have shared with each other?

- The risen Jesus joins the two, but they do not recognize him. What do you think it was that prevented them from recognizing Jesus?

- What do you make of the exchange of conversation between the two and Jesus?

- One of them says, " 'We had hoped that he [Jesus of Nazareth] was the one to redeem Israel.' " What do you think it was that had given them that hope?

- They report that some women of their group had astounded them with the news that they had found the tomb empty and had had a vision of angels who said that Jesus was alive. Why do you suppose the two have left Jerusalem in light of such news?

- The text reads, "Beginning with Moses and all the prophets, he interpreted to them the things about himself in all the scriptures." What are some of the things Jesus might have shared with the two?

- The two invite Jesus to stay with them because it is almost evening, and they share a meal together. What do you think of Jesus' assuming the role of host of the meal?

- Jesus blessed the bread and broke it and gave it to them. Then their eyes were opened, and they recognized him, and before they could exchange another word, Jesus vanished. What do you suppose Luke is trying to communicate in this part of the narrative?

- The two said, " 'Were not our hearts burning within us . . . while he was opening the scriptures to us?' " When is a time when you have experienced your heart burning within you when reading or hearing the Scriptures?

- Luke reports, "That same hour they got up and returned to Jerusalem." It was getting late in the day. Jerusalem was seven miles away, so it would take at least two hours to get there and probably longer in the dark. If they had any conversation along the way, what are some things you imagine them saying to each other?

- Imagine in your mind's eye the greeting they received when they reported to the eleven and to other followers their experience on the road. Put yourself in their shoes. Speak as you imagine they did in sharing the news.

- Conclude by asking one more question: "What new insights have come to you regarding this familiar passage?"

Considering Jesus' Appearance to His Disciples

Ask your class members to form groups of three persons each. (If the numbers do not work out evenly, it is okay for one or two groups to have four persons, in which case two will focus on the same passage.) Guide the participants through the following process:

- Assign each person one of three passages: Luke 24:36–43; Luke 24:44–49; or Luke 24:50–53.

- They are to read their passage and imagine themselves as one of the disciples present when Jesus appears in their midst.

- As they read, they are to reflect on one question: "As a disciple of Jesus, what am I thinking and feeling right now as the risen Jesus is present with me?"

- After time for reading the brief passage and for reflecting on the question, ask the small groups to engage in conversation.

- They are to remain in their role as disciples at the time of Jesus' appearance and to talk about what they are thinking and feeling about this experience.

- After a few minutes of conversation, call everyone together and conclude the activity with one question: "What are some insights and impressions that have come to you as a result of what you experienced the last few minutes?"

Evaluating the Course

Take a few minutes with the group to share the following:

- We have spent a number of weeks together studying Luke's Gospel. We have read the Participant's Guide and many passages in Luke, we have participated in a variety of activities together, and we have discussed many questions. It is impossible to remember all we have said and done together, but I am sure there are some things that are memorable from our study. Let's take a few minutes to reflect on our experience of Luke's Gospel.

- Of all the activities we did together, which ones were the most interesting, challenging, or helpful for you?

- What are some suggestions you would make regarding a future study like this one?

- What are some questions that have been provoked in your mind about the life and ministry of Jesus from the perspective of Luke's Gospel?

- The author of the Participant's Guide poses two questions at the end of chapter 7: "How has Luke instructed you?" "How has Luke helped you become a more faithful disciple?"

Closing

Toward the end of chapter 7 the author of the Participant's Guide writes, "Now is the time to play the last movement of Beethoven's Ninth Symphony—the 'Ode to Joy.' Note the way Luke, the great literary artist, has punctuated the end of his story: *Worship! Joy! Thanksgiving!*" This would be a great way to conclude the session and the course. Obtain from your own collection, the local library, or from the iTunes store the "Ode to Joy."

After listening to the recording, give the participants a minute to think or write a completion to a sentence that begins, "Luke has helped me to understand. . . ." Then invite participants to share their sentences, and in response to each sentence everyone will say in unison the opening words of the hymn based on the "Ode to Joy": "Joyful, joyful, we adore thee, God of glory, Lord of love."

Appendix

Commentaries on Luke

Culpepper, R. Alan. "The Gospel of Luke," *The New Interpreter's Bible*, Vol. 9. Nashville: Abingdon Press, 1995.

Fitzmyer, Joseph A. *The Gospel according to Luke*, 2 vols. Garden City, NY: Doubleday, 1981.

Powell, Mark Allan. *What Are They Saying about Luke?* New York: Paulist Press, 1989.

Ringe, Sharon H. *Luke*. Westminster Bible Companion. Louisville, KY: Westminster John Knox Press, 1995.

Tannehill, Robert C. *Luke*. Abingdon New Testament Commentaries. Nashville: Abingdon Press, 1996.

Bible Study Aids

Achtemeier, Paul J., gen. ed. *The HarperCollins Bible Dictionary*. San Francisco: HarperCollins Publishers in consultation with the Society of Biblical Literature, 1996.

Frank, Harry Thomas, ed. *Atlas of the Bible Lands: New Edition*. Union, NJ: Hammond World Atlas Corp., 2007.

Mays, James L., gen. ed. *The HarperCollins Bible Commentary*. San Francisco: HarperCollins Publishers in consultation with the Society of Biblical Literature, 2000.

Nelson's Complete Book of Bible Maps and Charts. Nashville: Thomas Nelson Publishers, 1996.

Study Bibles

The Access Bible (NRSV). New York: Oxford University Press, 1999.

> Features include introductory articles for each book of the Bible; sidebar essays, maps, and charts in places appropriate to the text; section-by-section commentaries on the text; a glossary; a brief concordance; and a section of Bible maps in color.

The Discipleship Study Bible: New Revised Standard Version, including Apocrypha. Louisville, KY: Westminster John Knox Press, 2008.

> Features include introductory articles for each book of the Bible, study notes for key portions of each chapter of the Bible, a concise concordance, and helpful maps.

The Learning Bible (CEV). New York: American Bible Society, 2000.

> Features include introductory articles and outlines for each book of the Bible; fifteen background articles and over one hundred miniarticles; charts and timelines; a miniatlas; notes on biblical texts in six categories, each identified by a different color and symbol (geography; people and nations; objects, plants, and animals; ideas and concepts; history and culture; and cross-references); and hundreds of illustrations, photographs, and diagrams in color.

The New Interpreter's Study Bible: New Revised Standard Version with Apocrypha. Nashville: Abingdon Press, 2003.

> Features include introductory articles for each book of the Bible, extensive textual notes, many excursus essays, a helpful glossary, general articles related to biblical authority and interpretation, and colorful maps.

The NIV Study Bible (NIV). Grand Rapids: Zondervan, 1985.

> Features include introductory articles and outlines for each book of the Bible; extensive notes for explanation and interpretation of the biblical text on each page; helpful charts, maps, diagrams within the biblical text; an index to subjects; a concise concordance; and a collection of maps in color.